Hello Coloring Book Fans!

Welcome to my 5th adult coloring book, Hoot Owls!

I have illustrated and designed for you 40 single-sided cute Hoot Owl patterns to color! This coloring book is my 5th coloring book for adults! There is a variety of fun and challenging designs to color. Some of the patterns are more complex than others.
Hoot Owls offers hours of relaxing adult coloring fun! I have included a test page so you can test out your pencils, crayons, gel pens or whatever medium you choose.

Thank you for purchasing my adult coloring book,
Hoot Owls!

I would like to thank the best boyfriend in the world, Brian Dages for his support! xoxo

Thank you to all who have purchased my previous 4 coloring books!

Suzanne Lapila - Illustrator - Author

Please like my:
Facebook page: Coloring Books By Suzy
Instagram: suzys_adult_coloring_books
My blog: suzysadultcoloringbooks.blogspot.com

email contact: suzyl22@aol.com

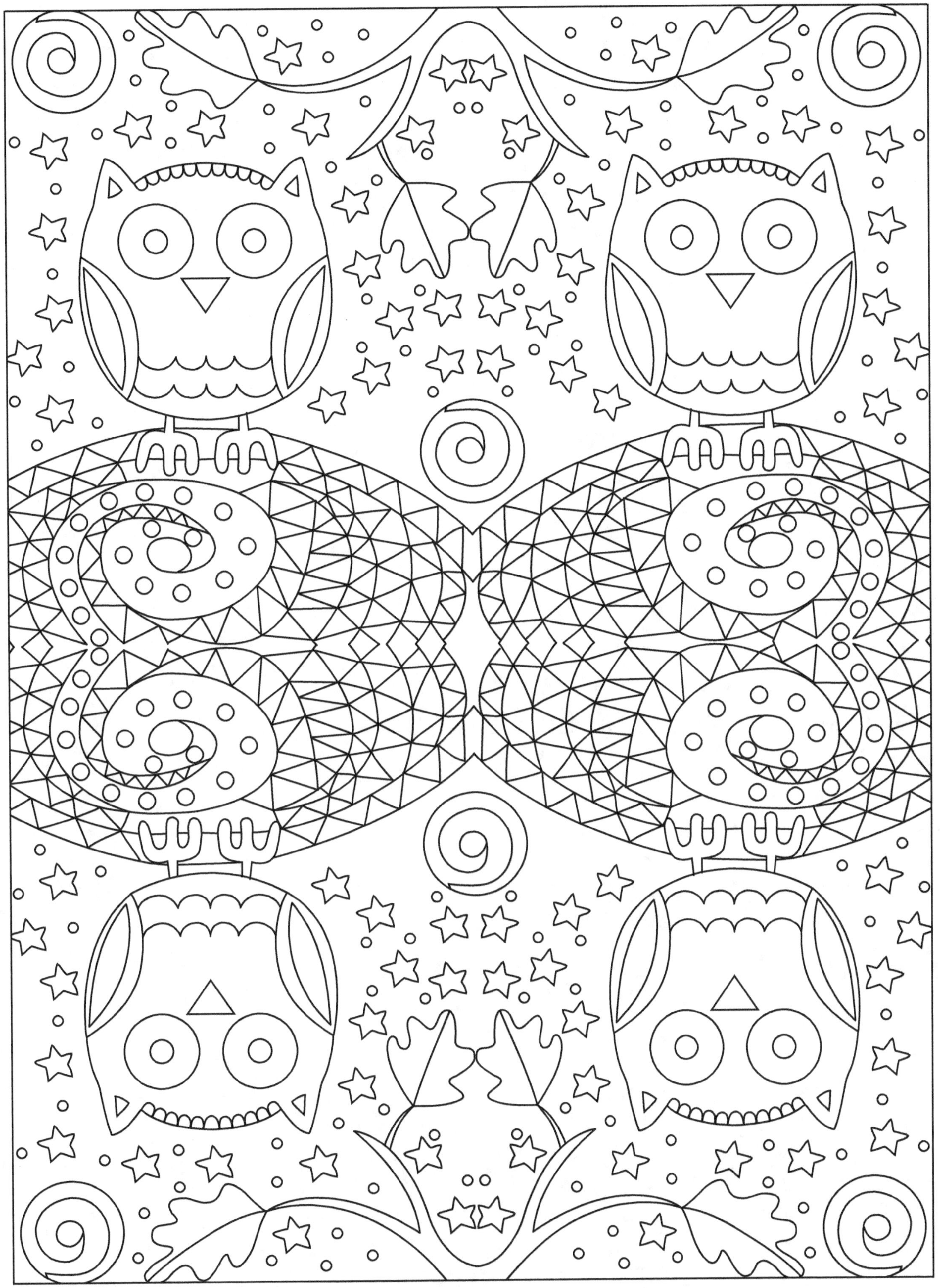

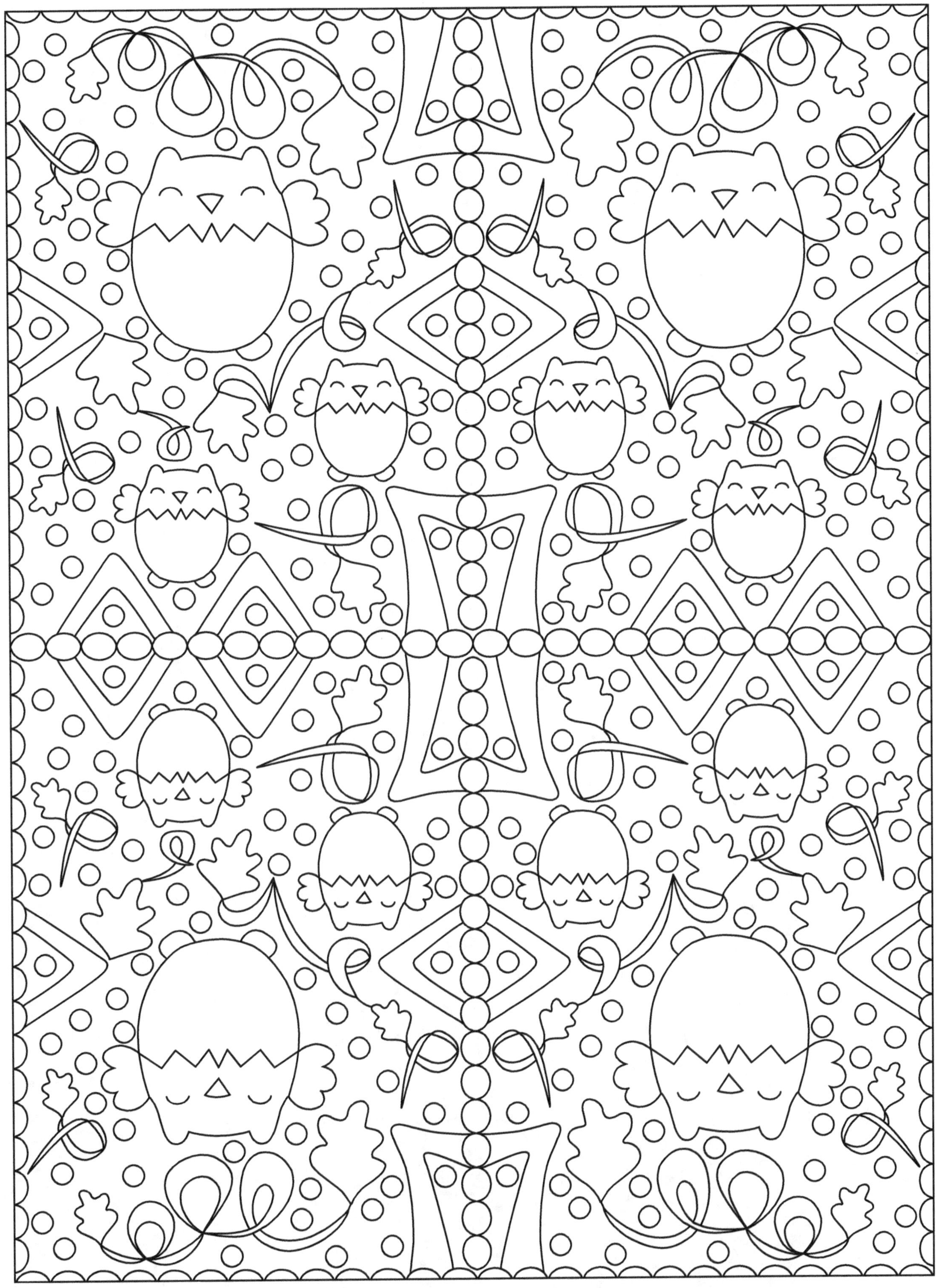

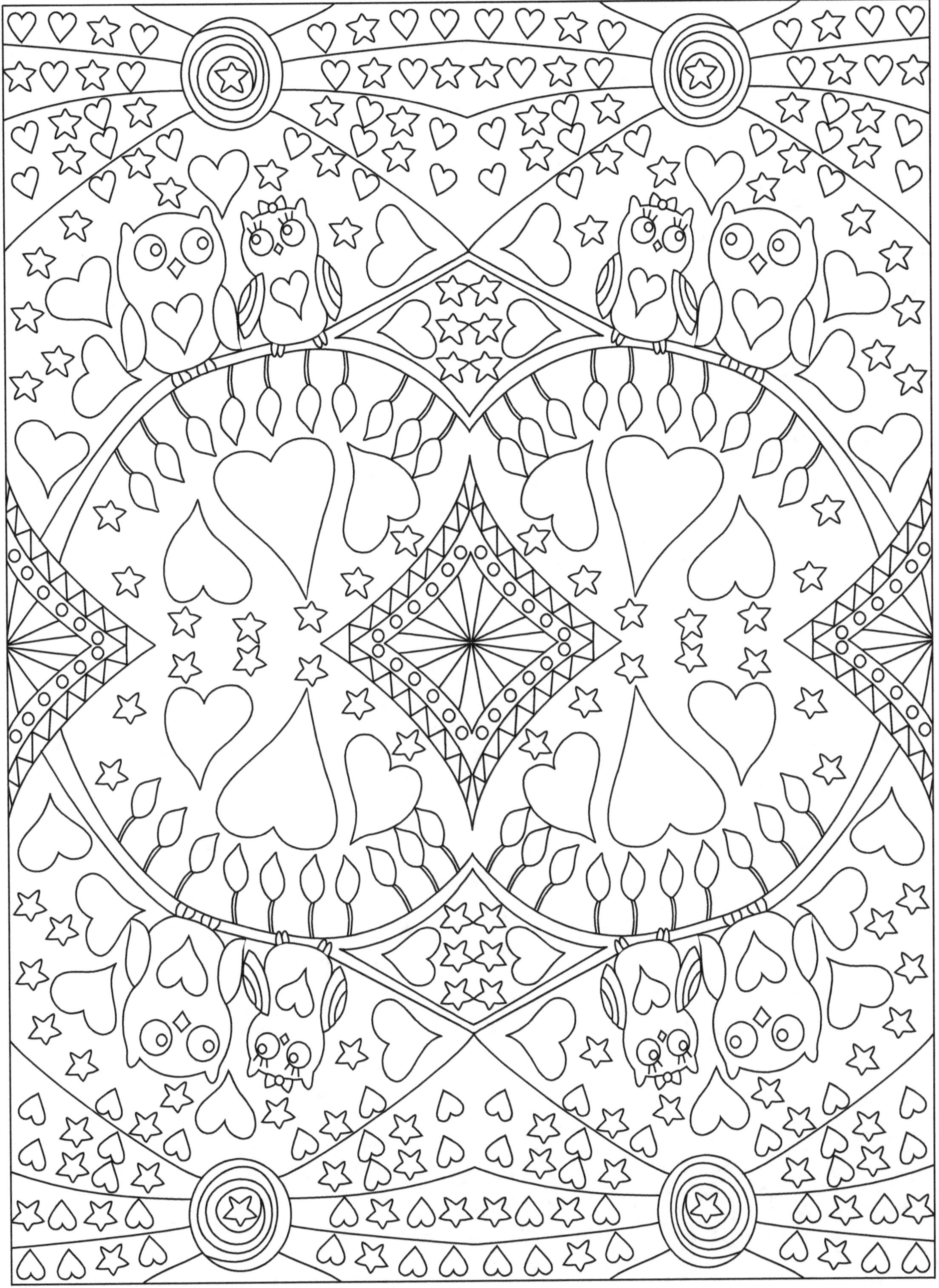

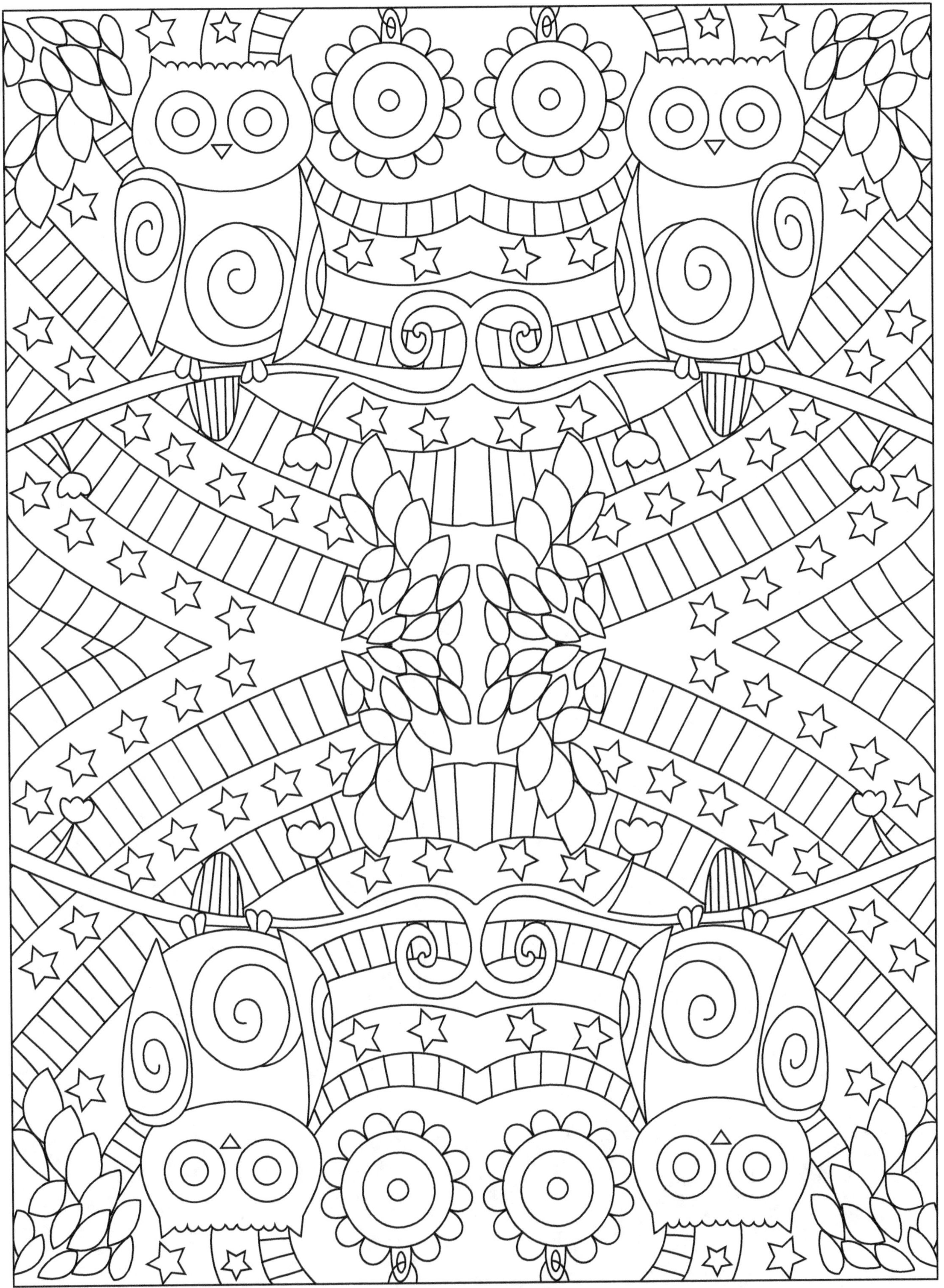

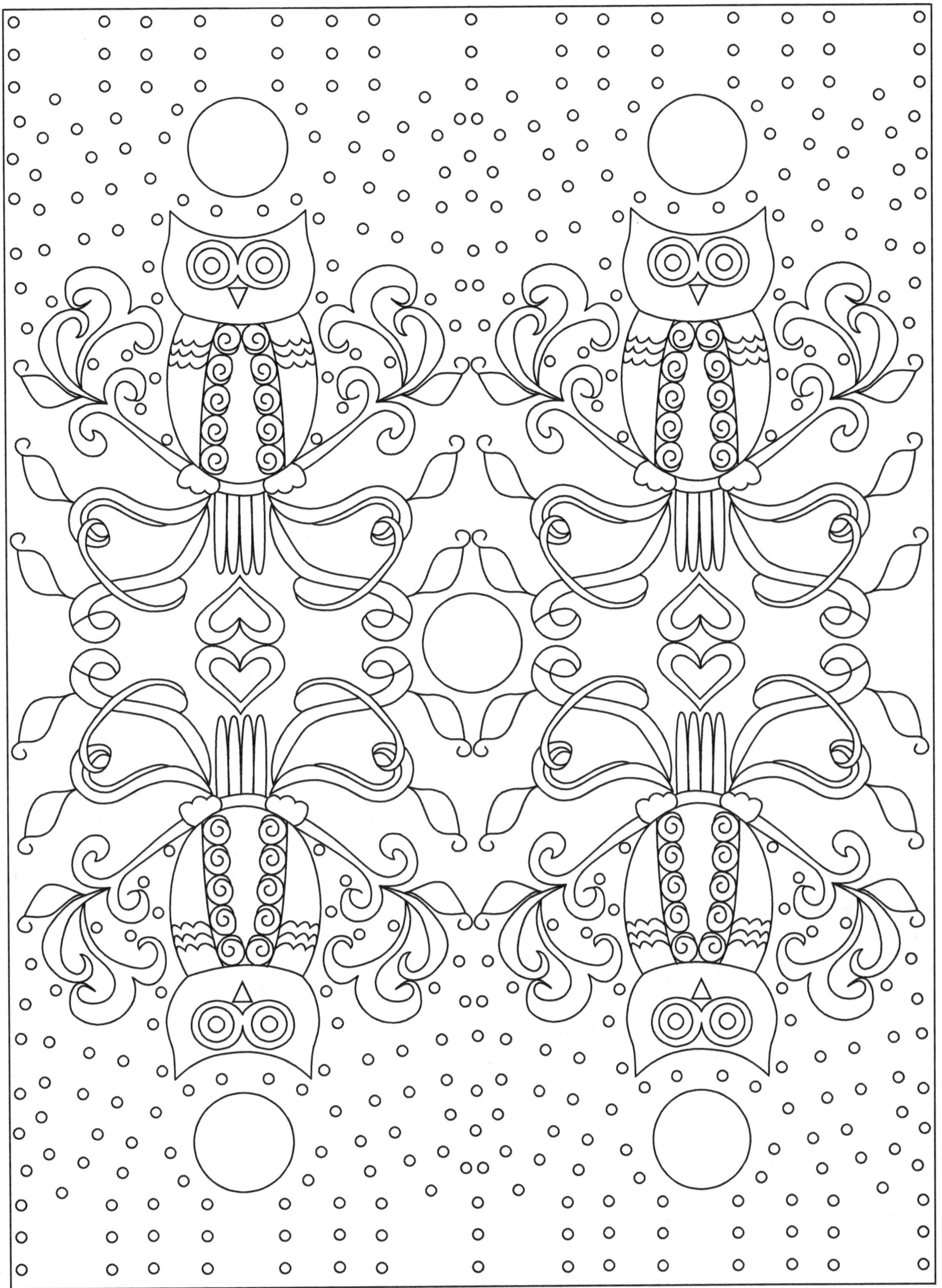

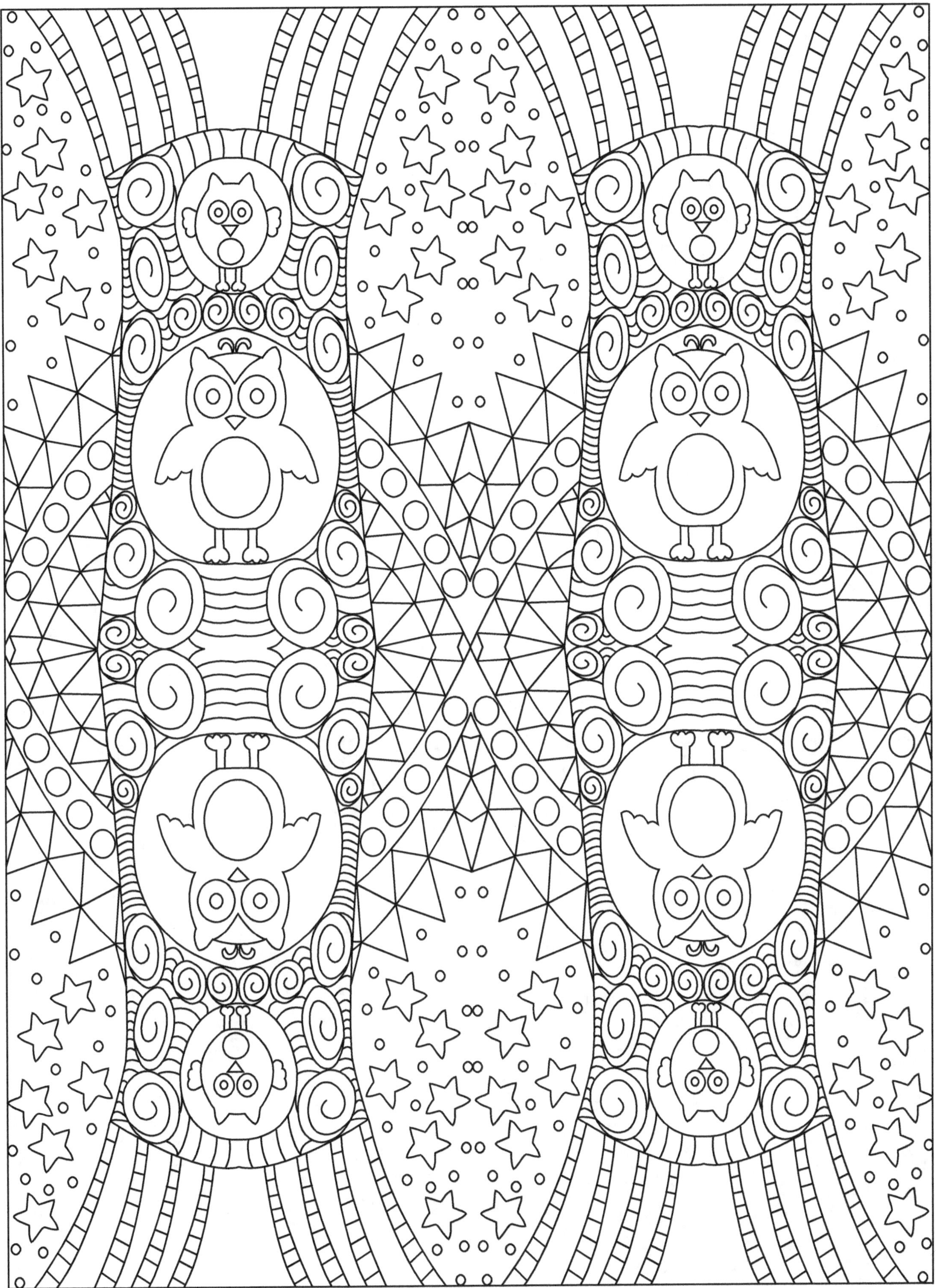

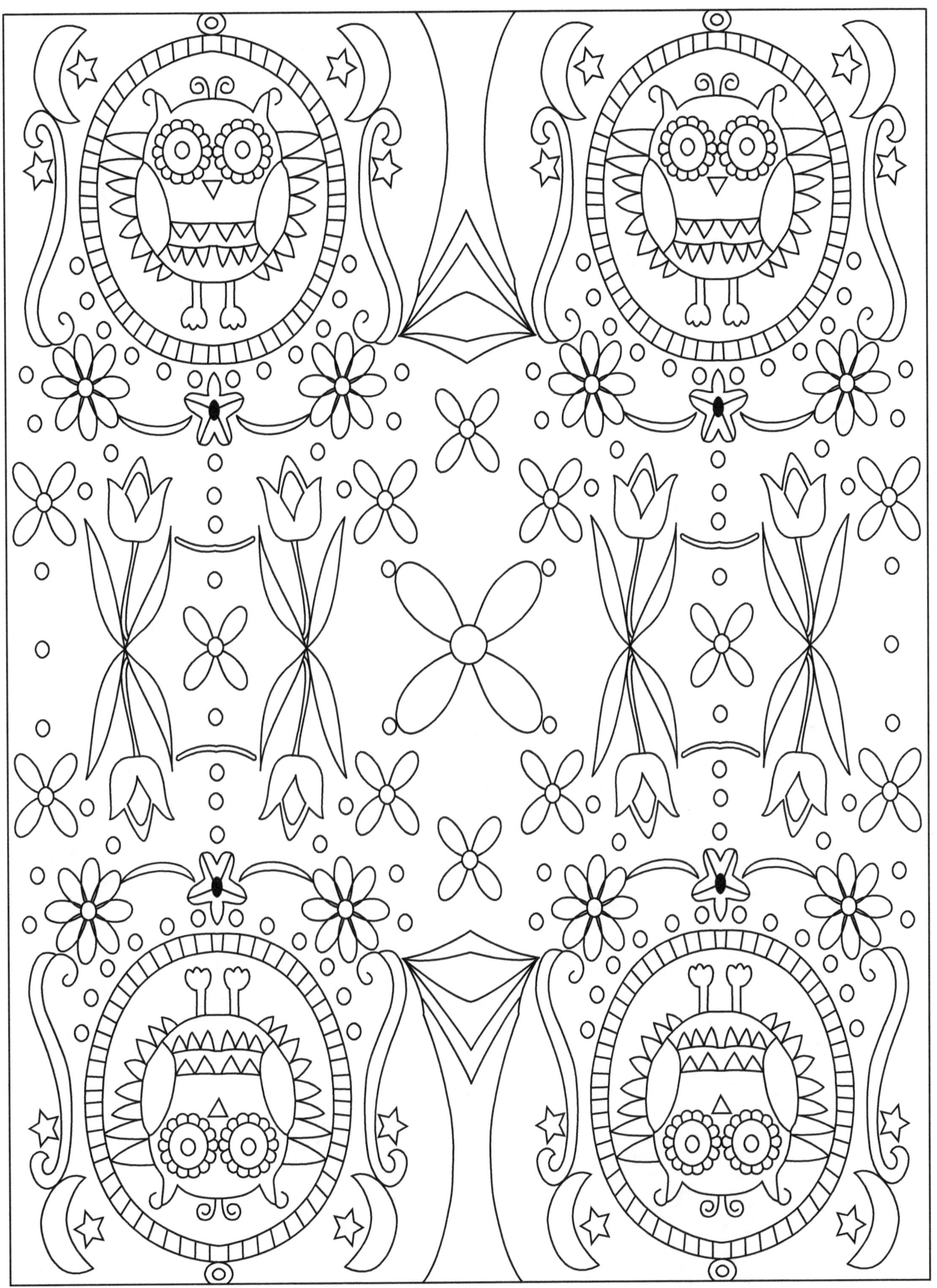

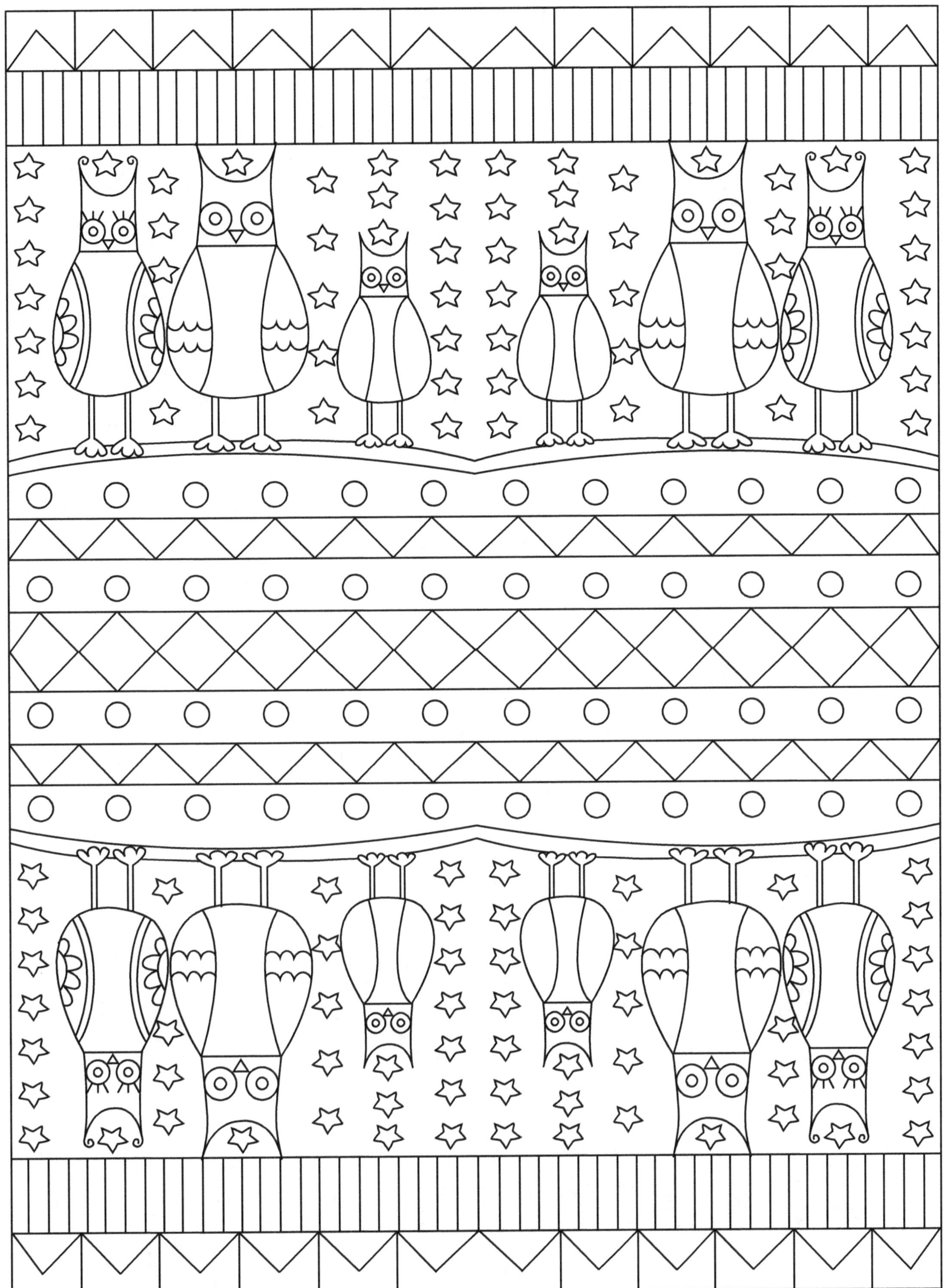

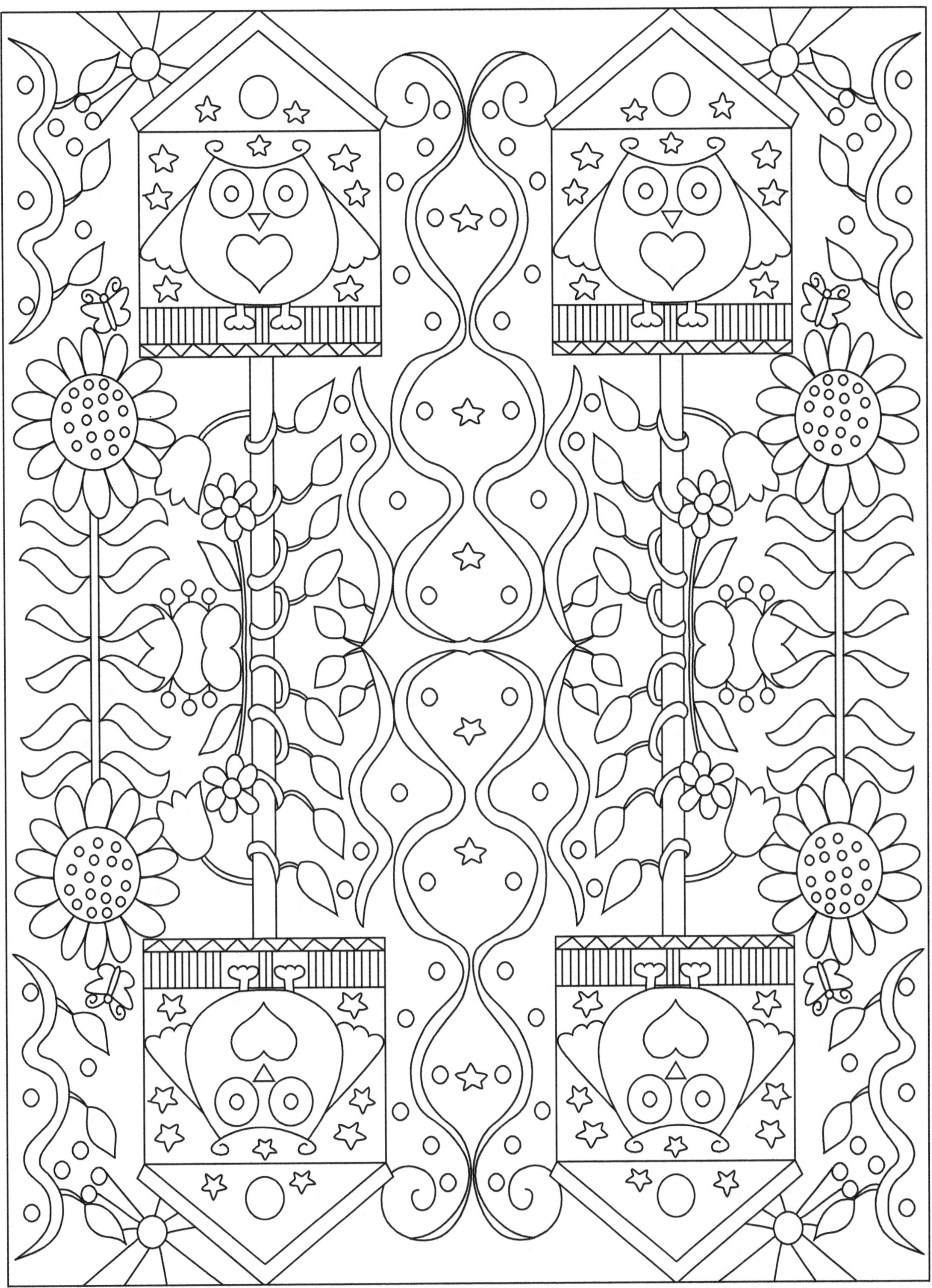

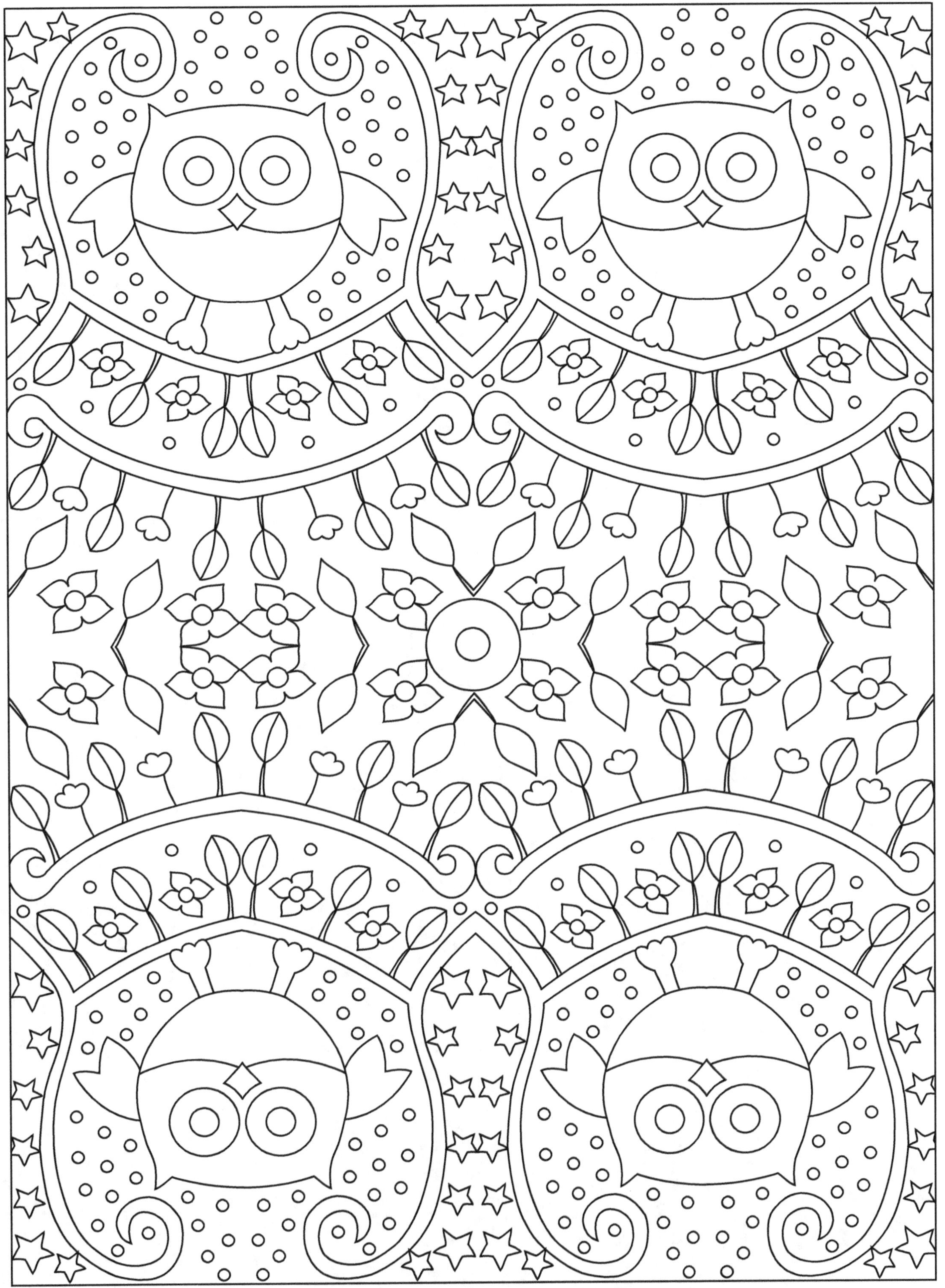

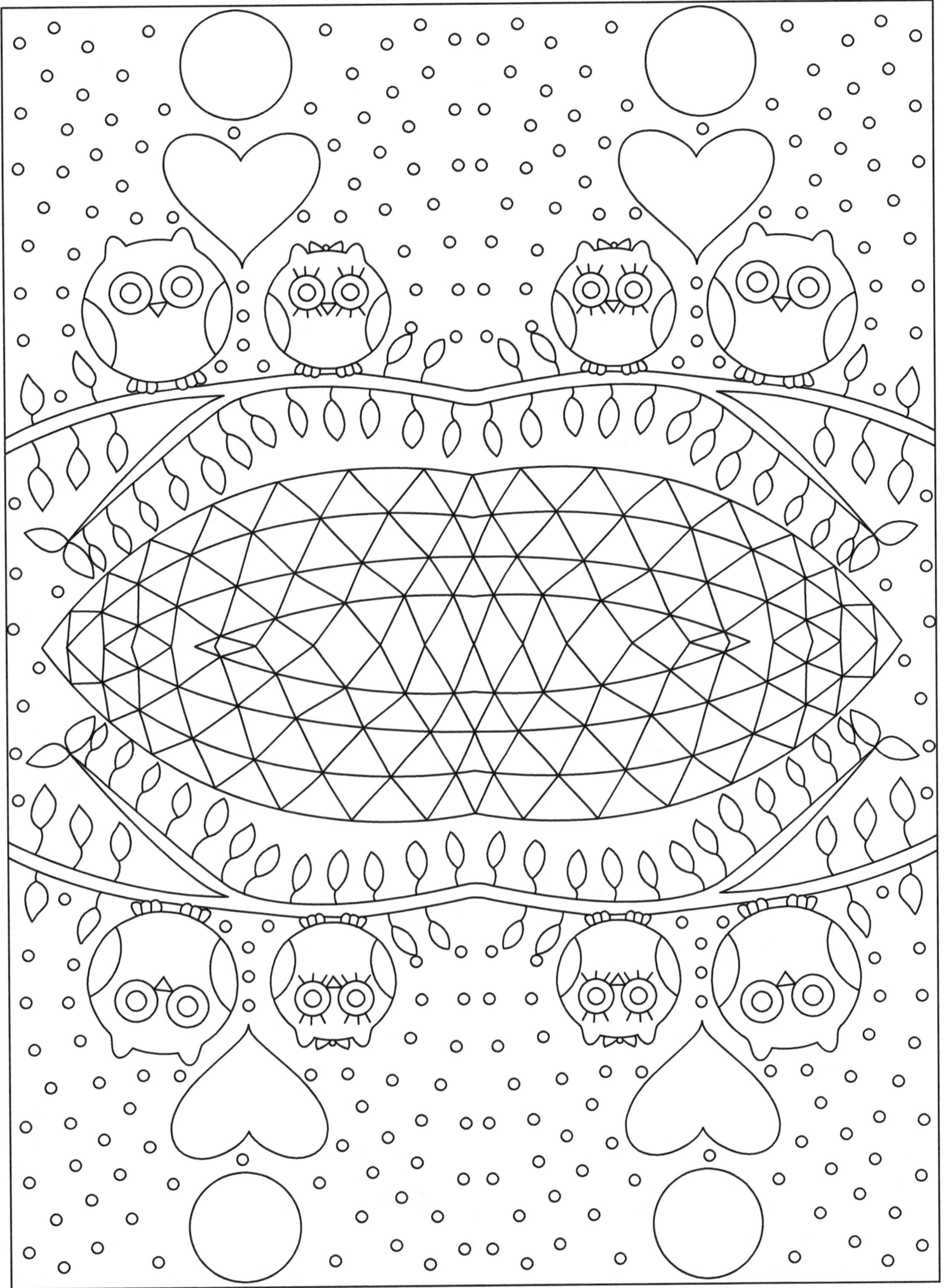

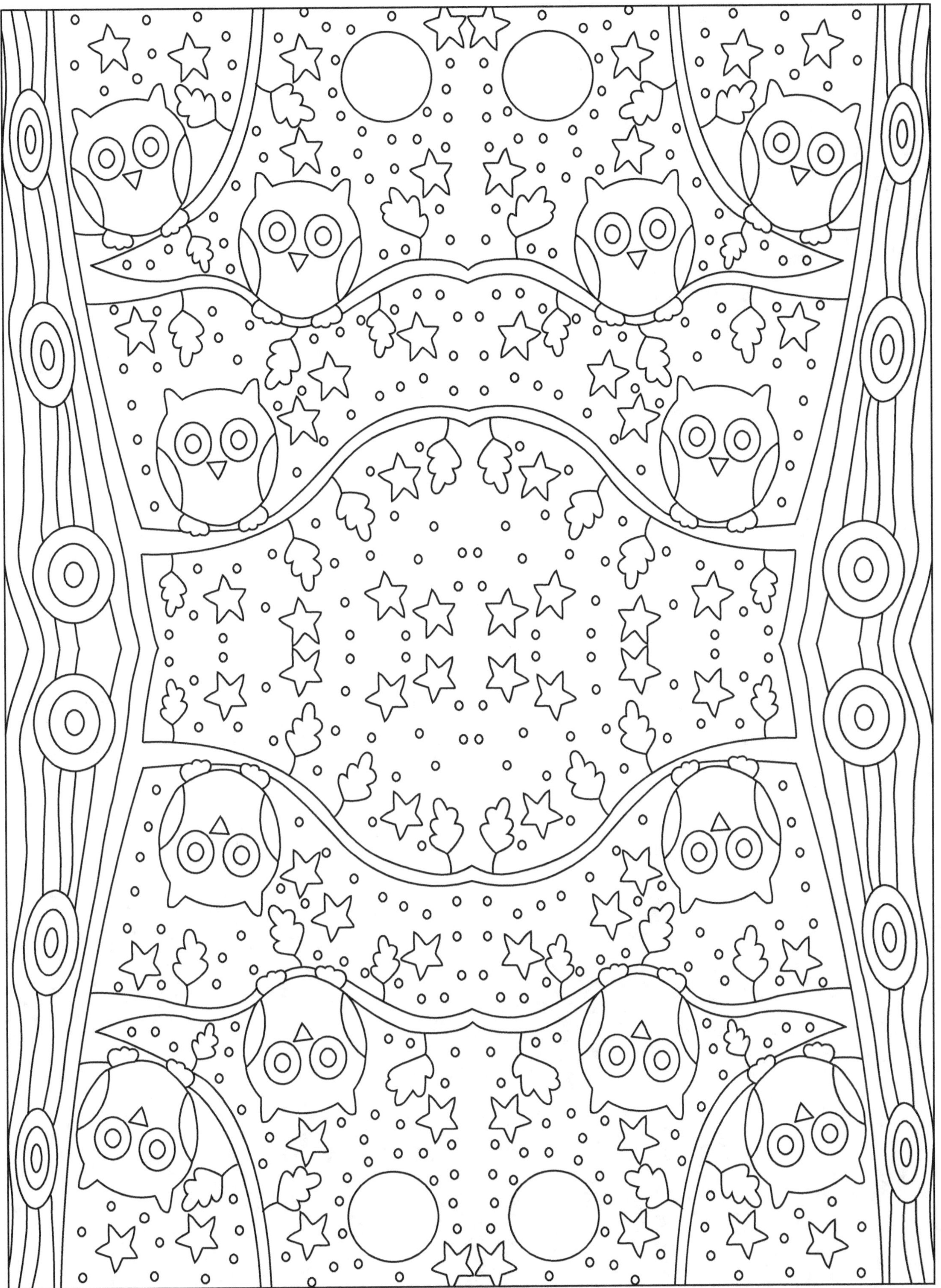

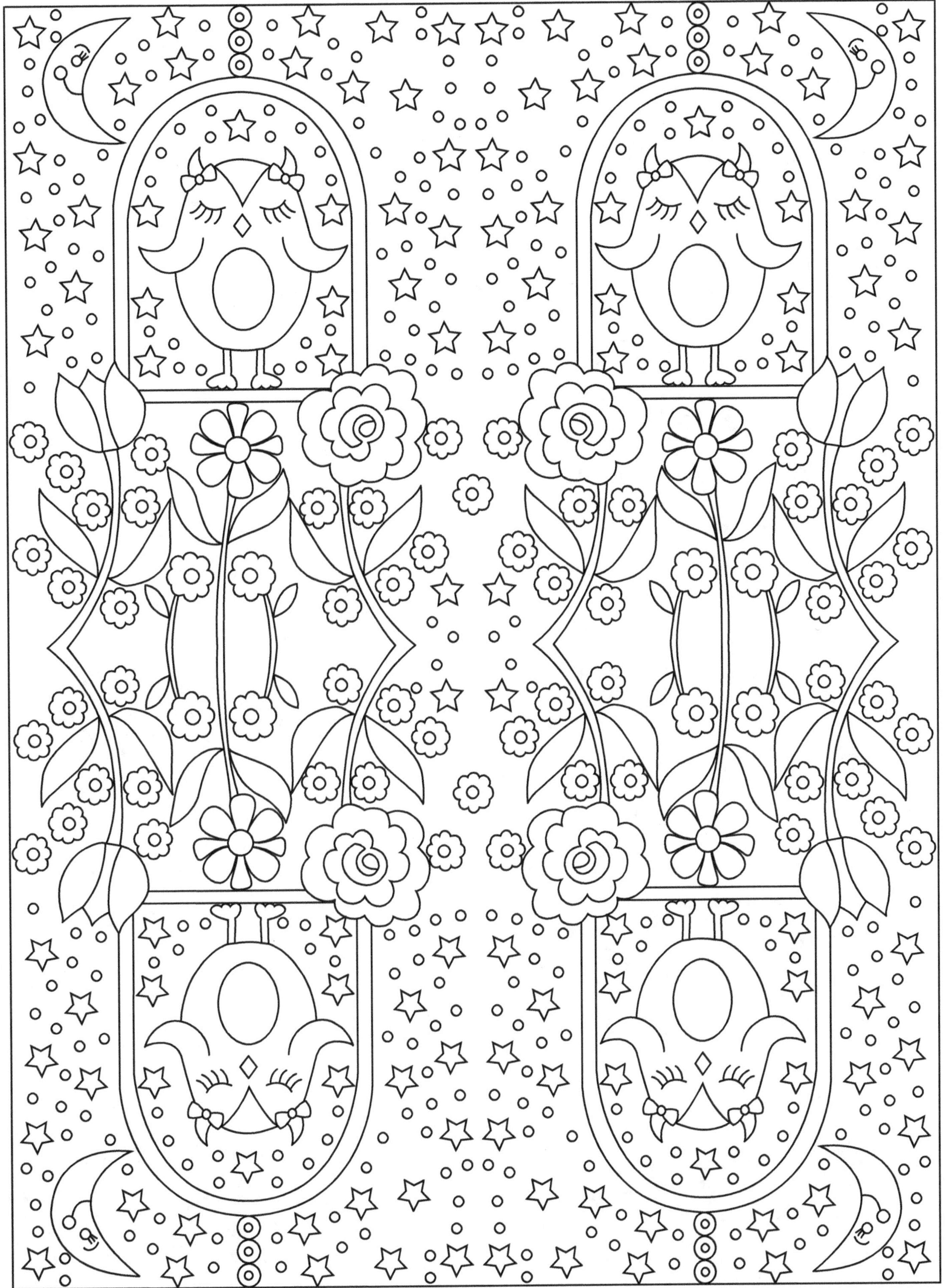

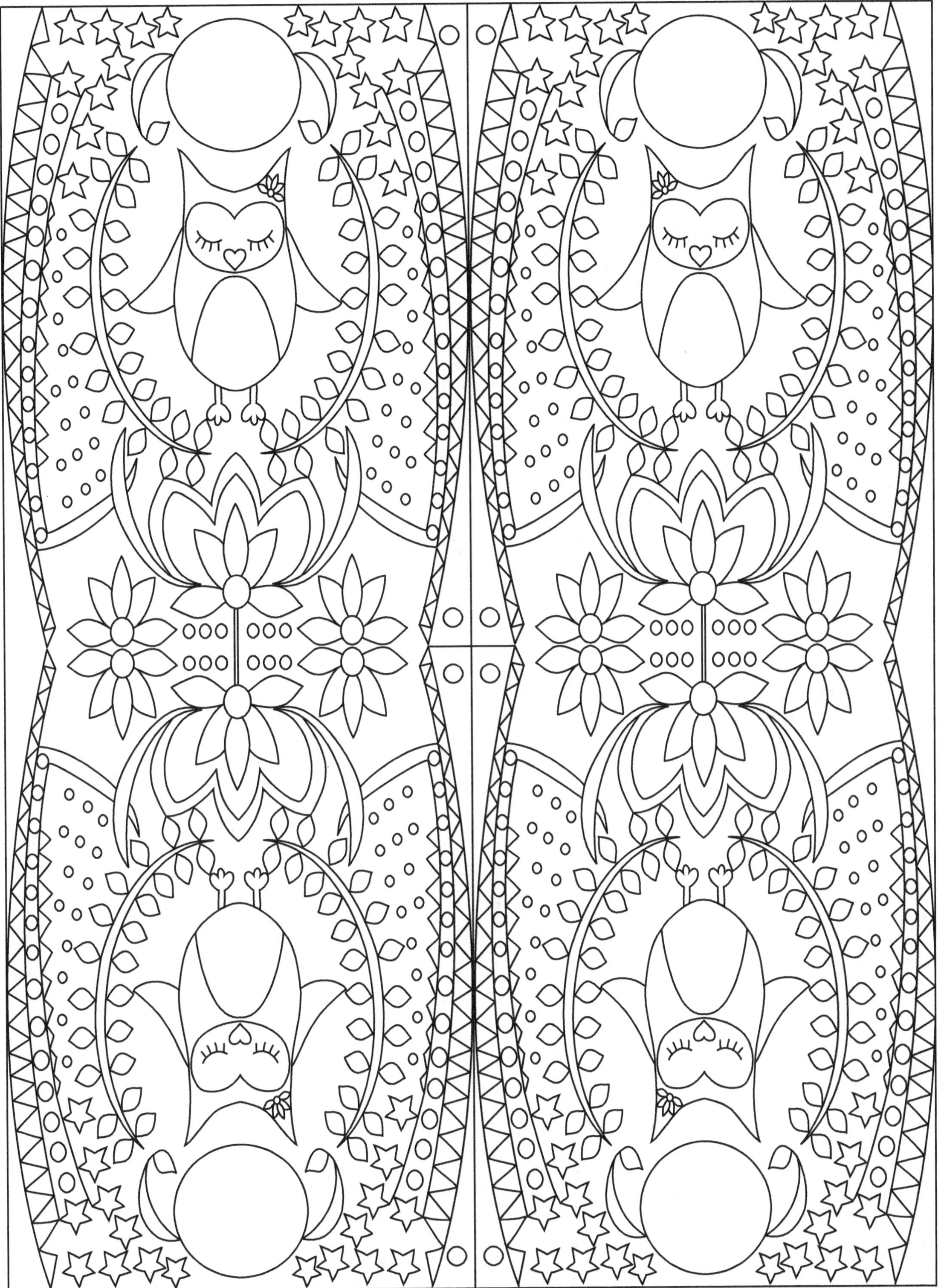

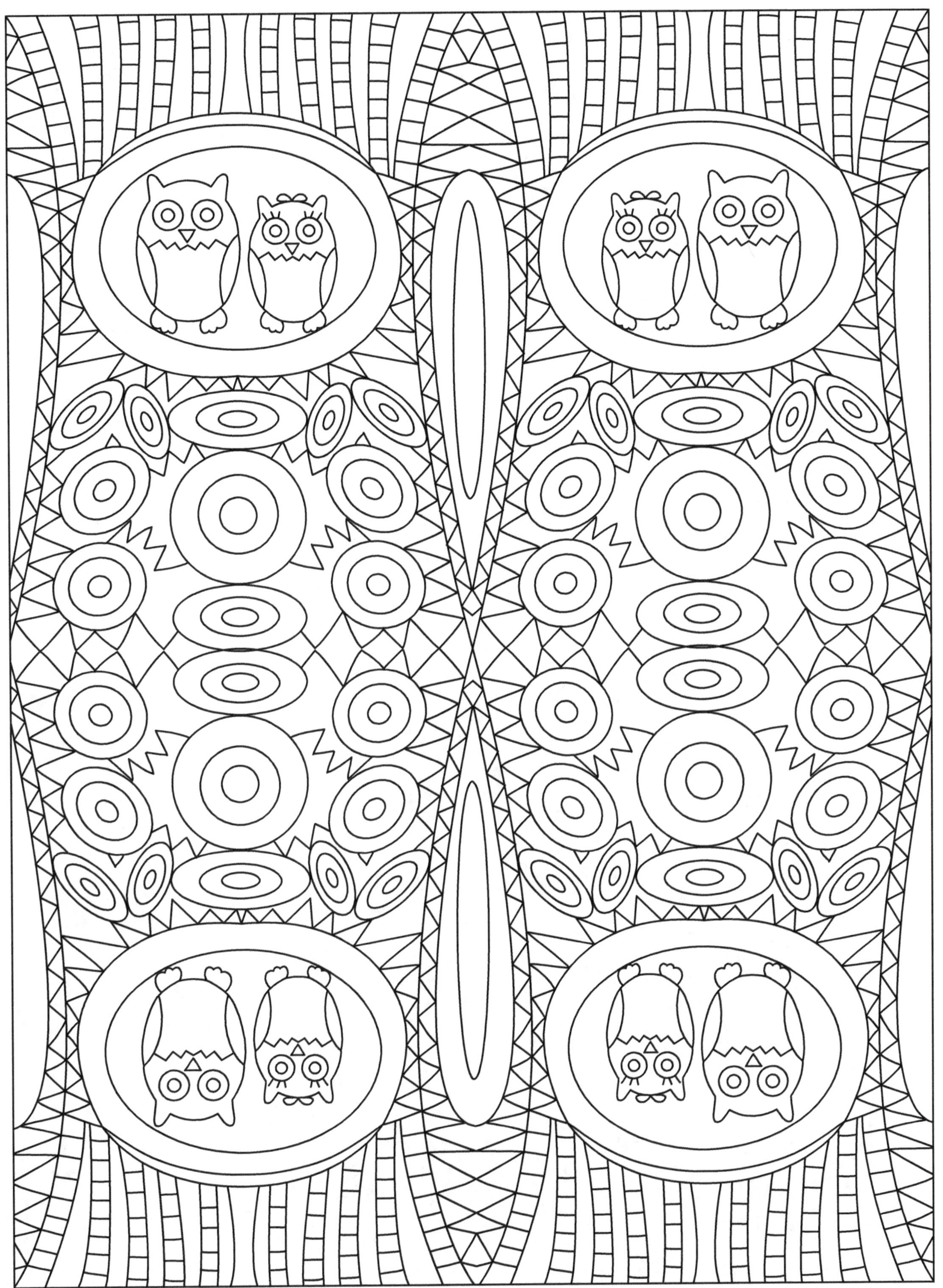

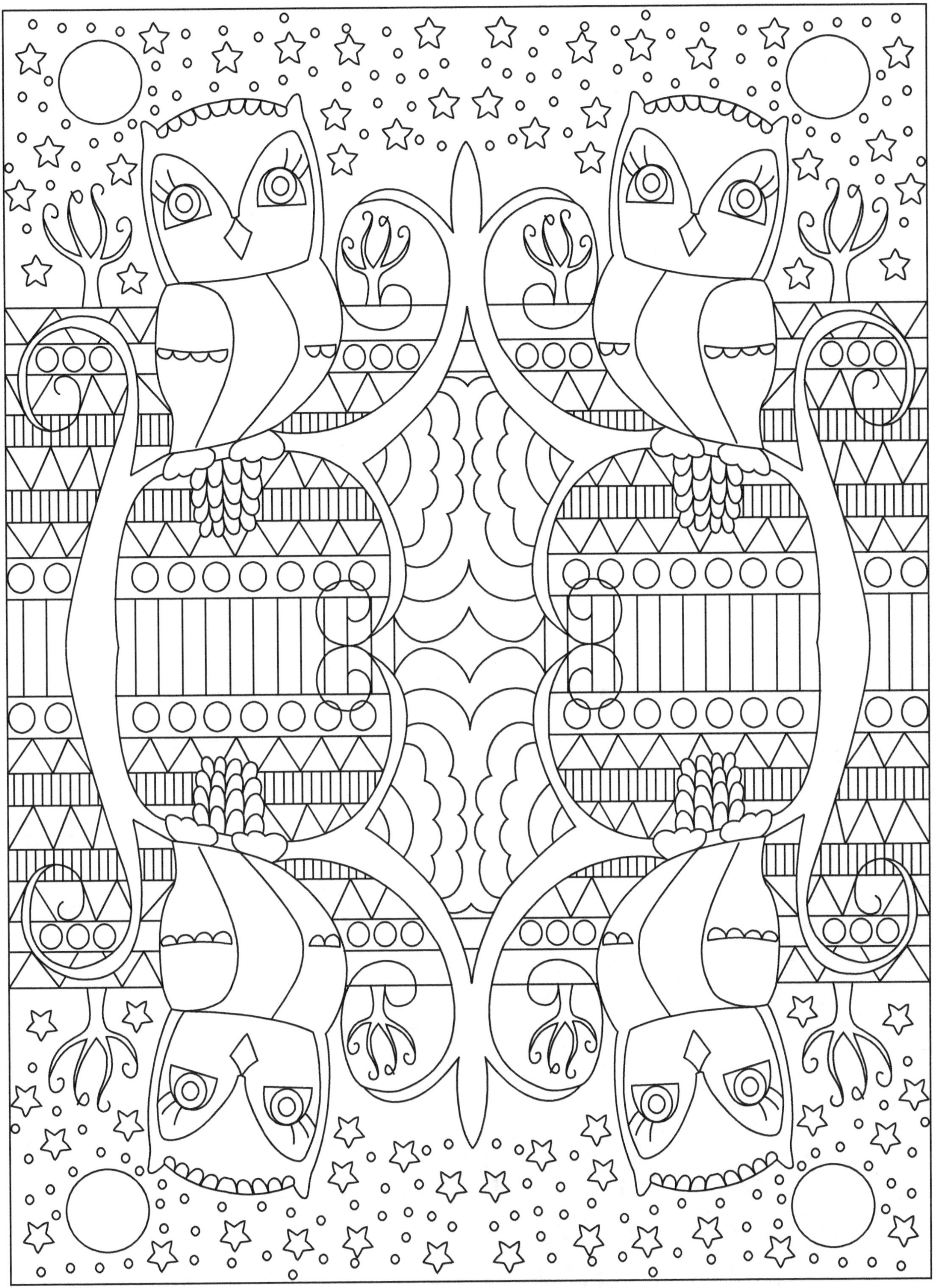

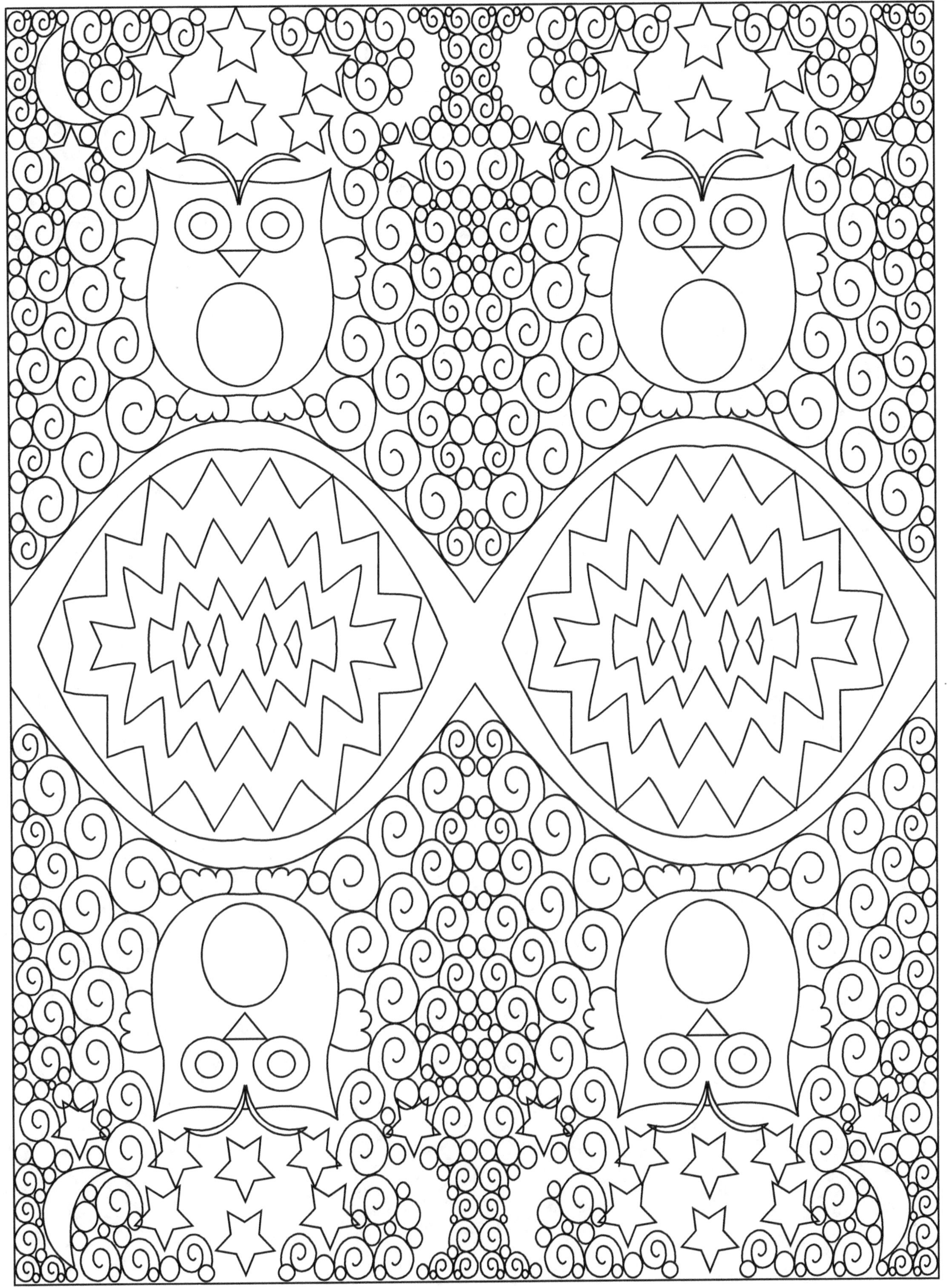

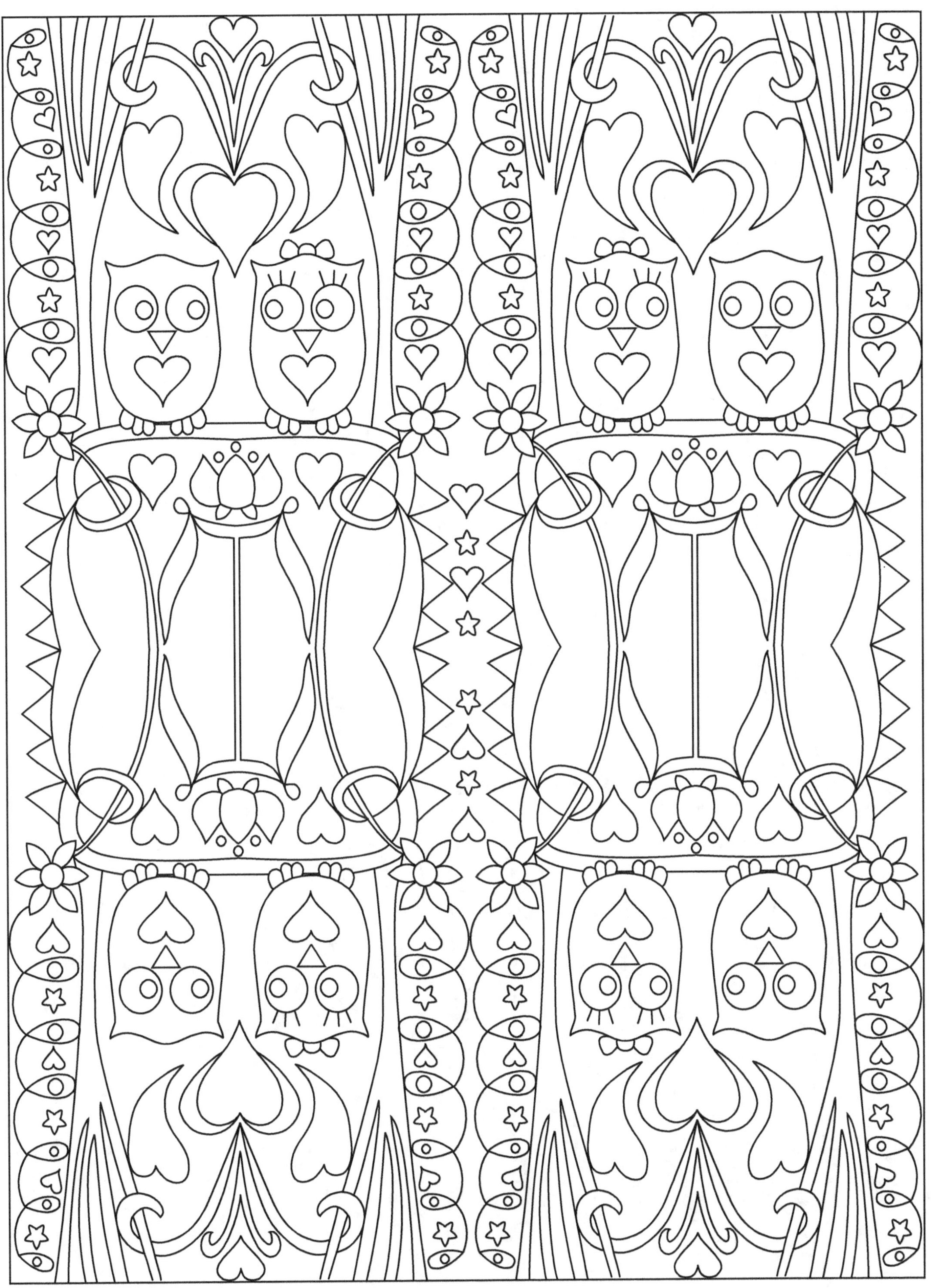

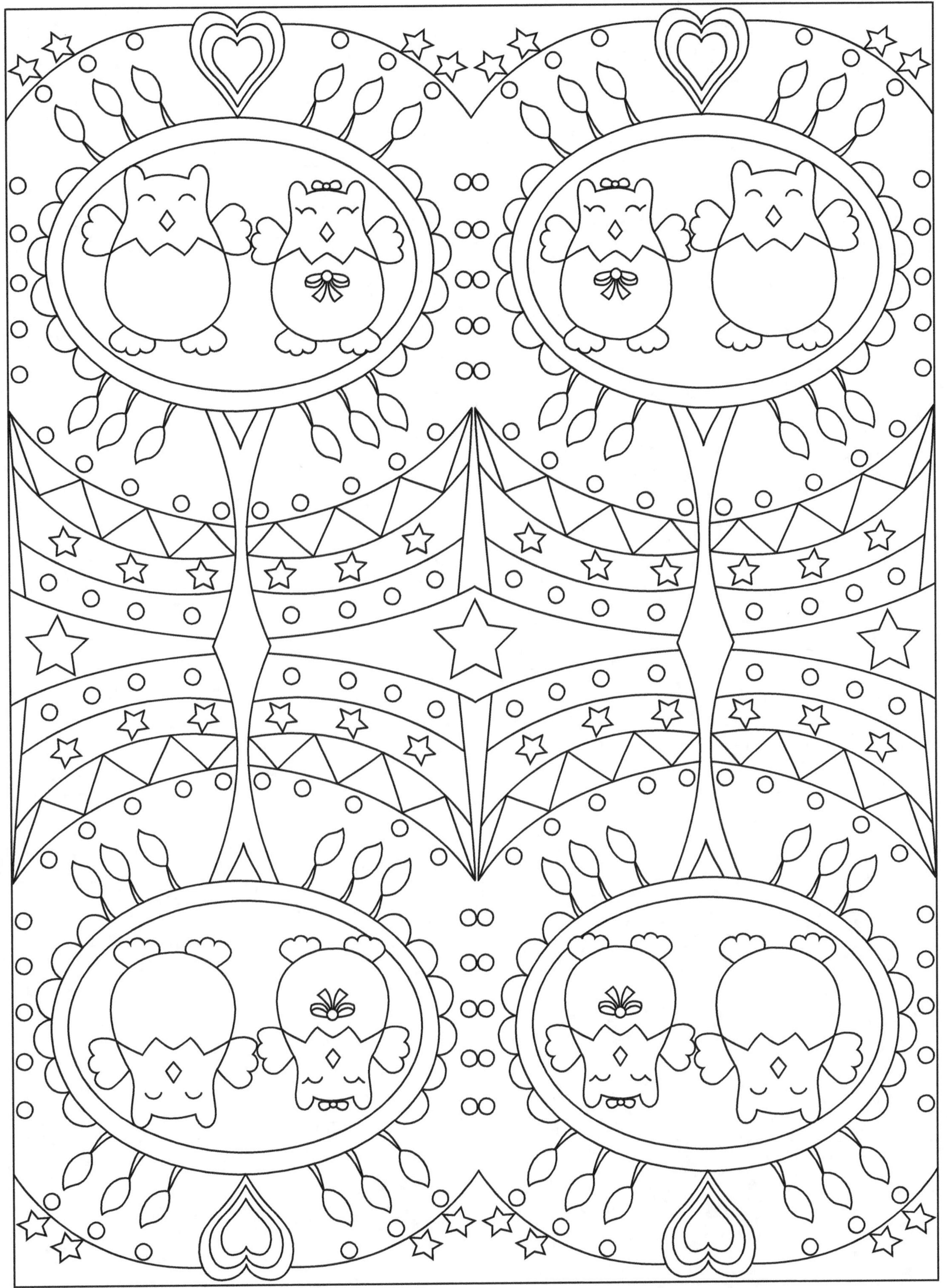

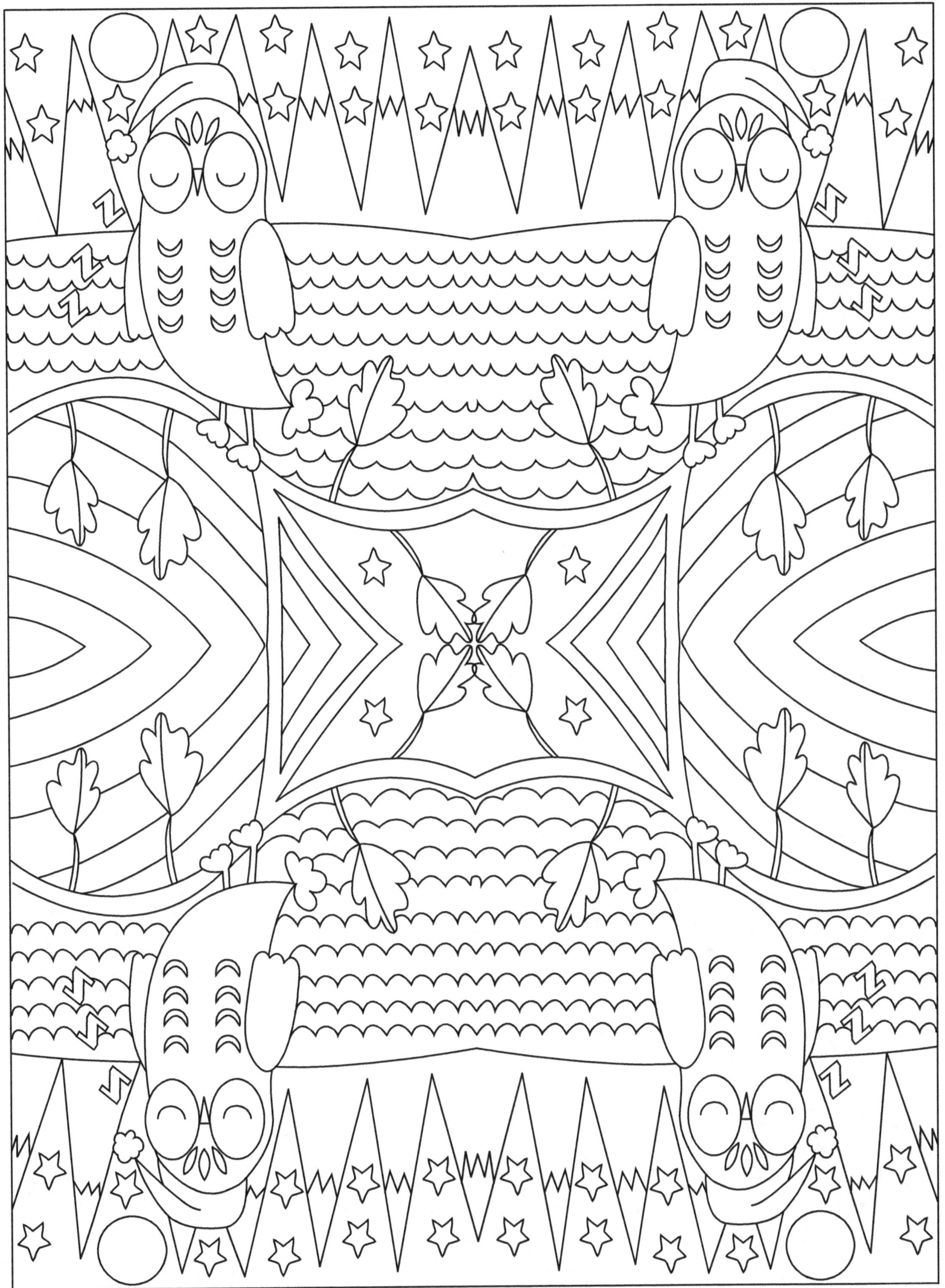

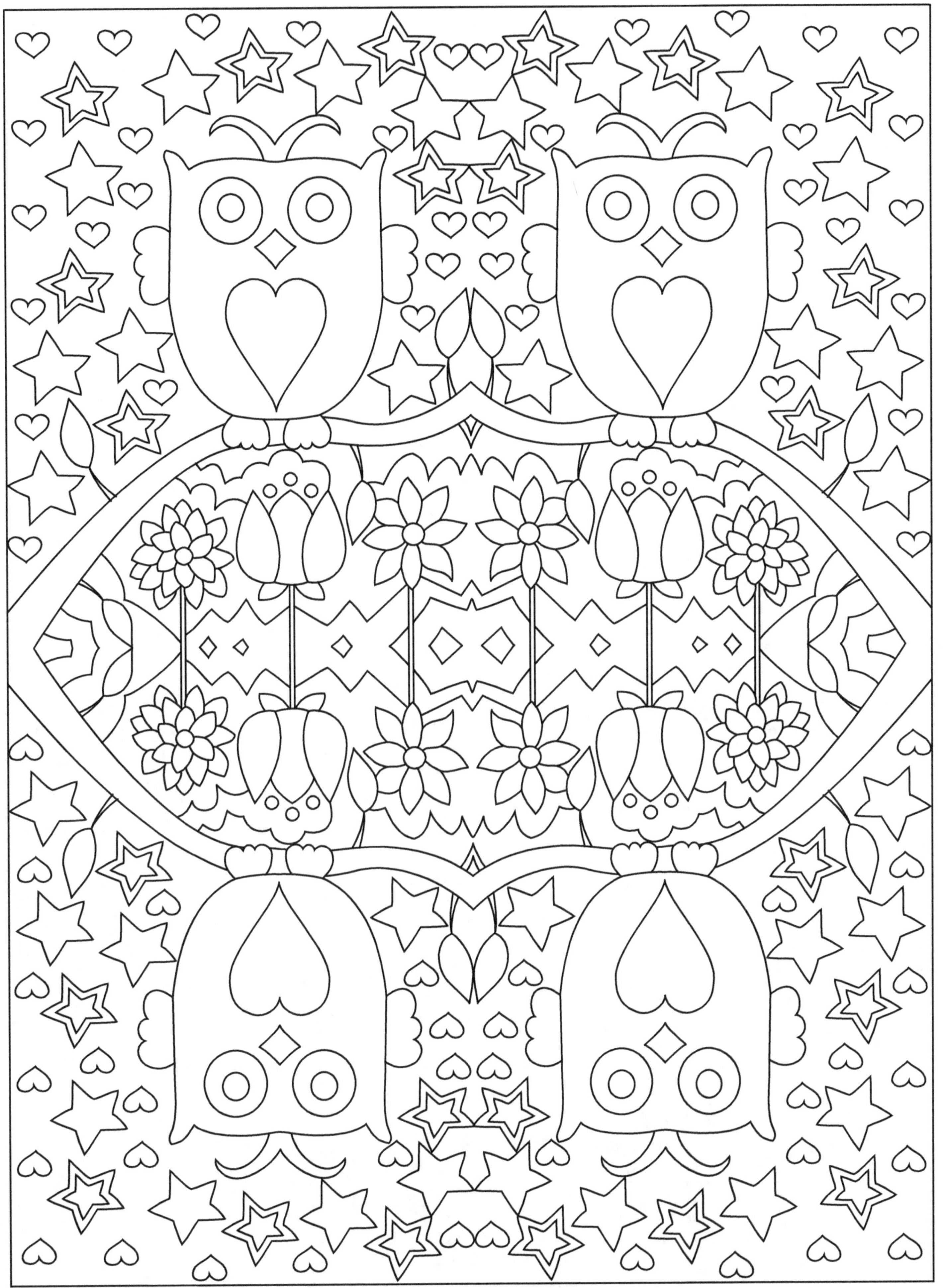

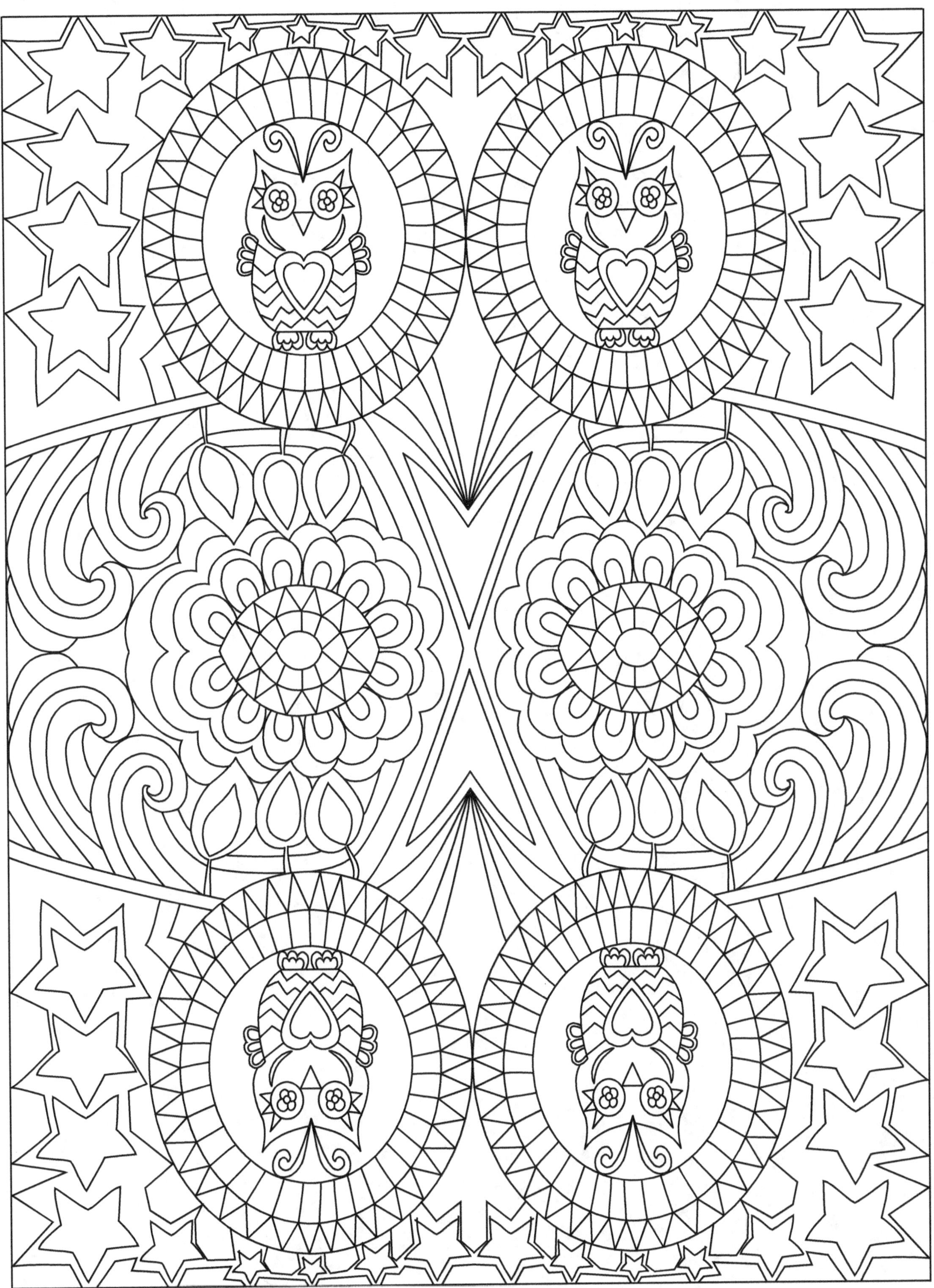

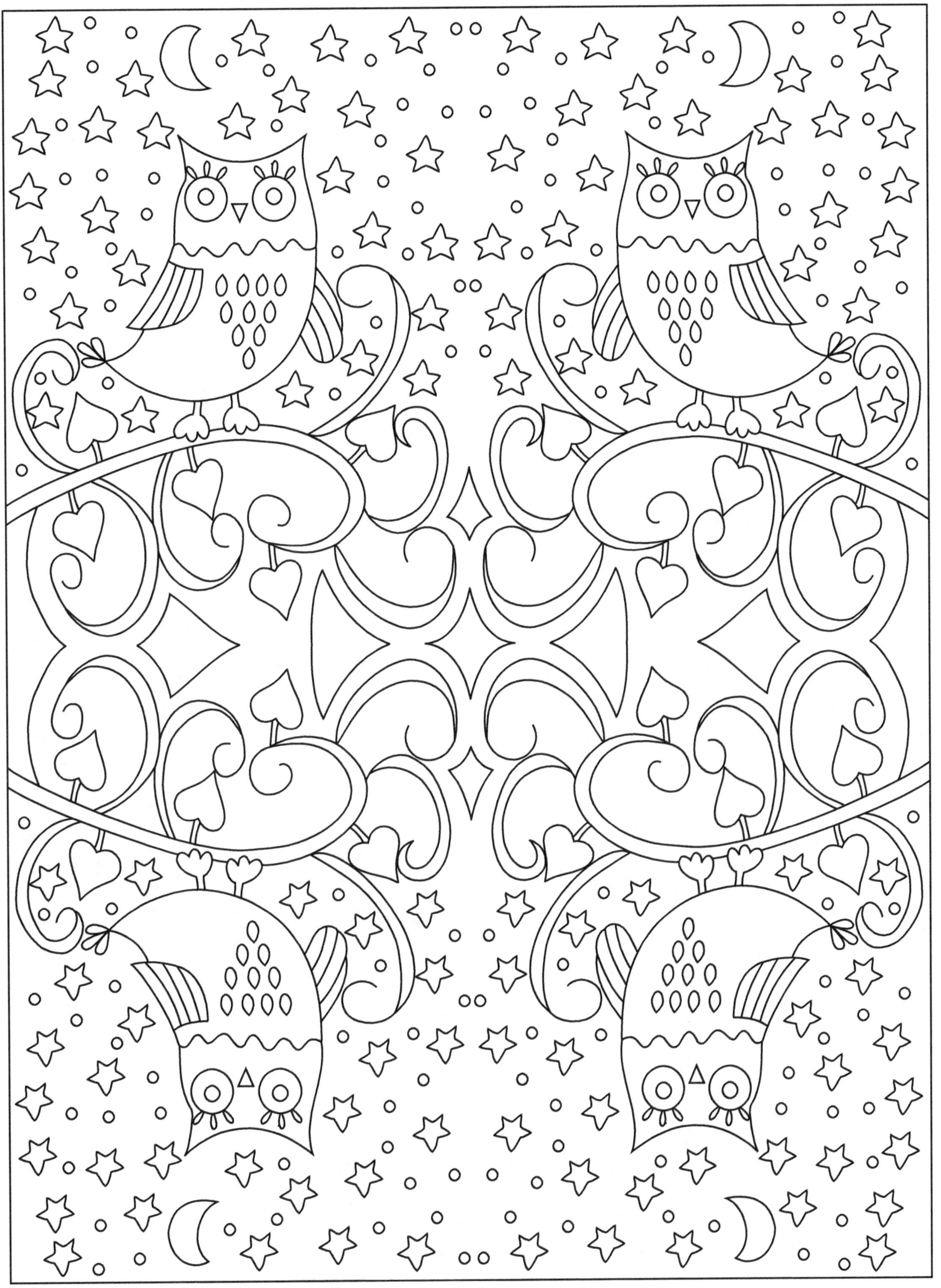

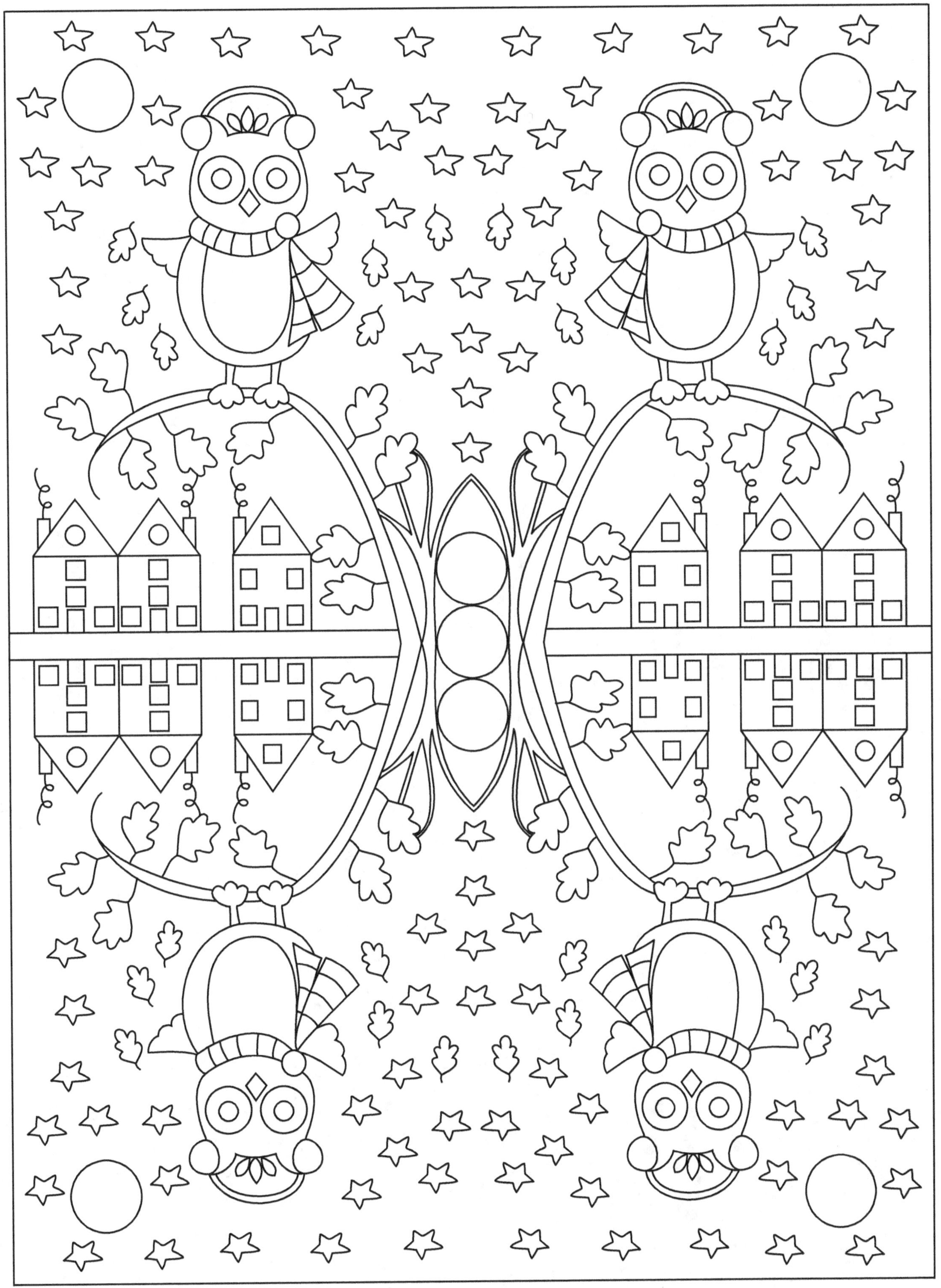

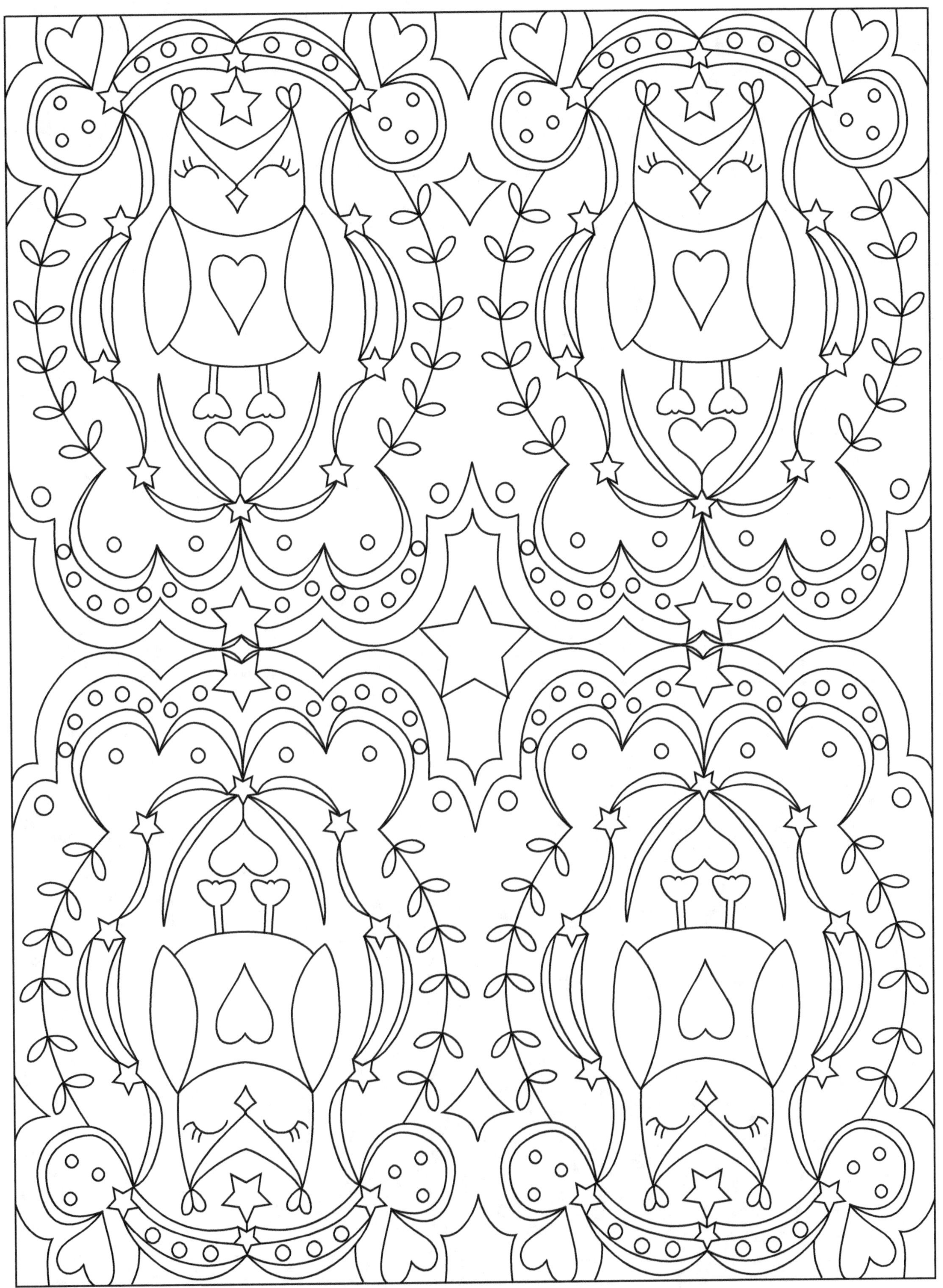

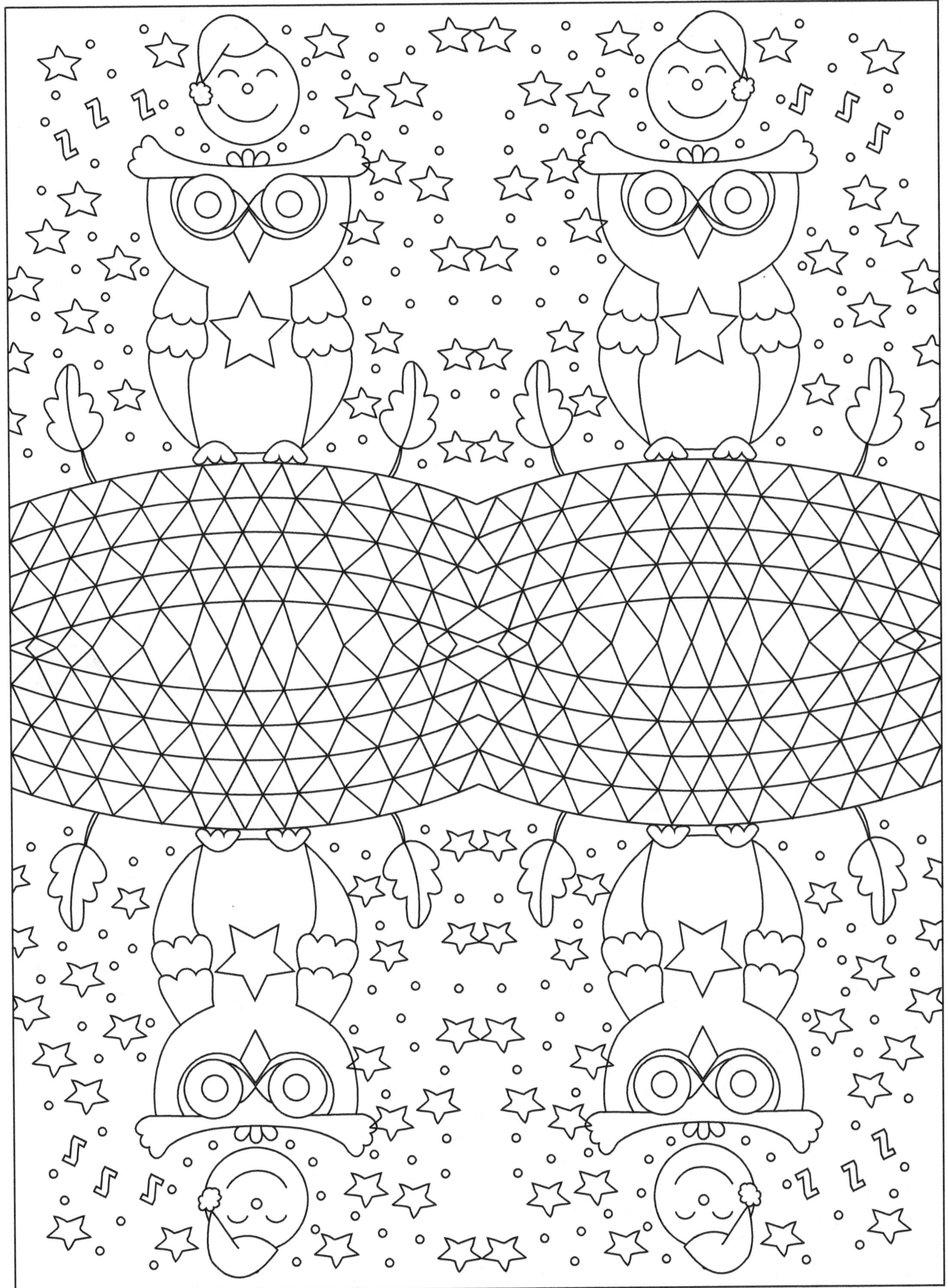

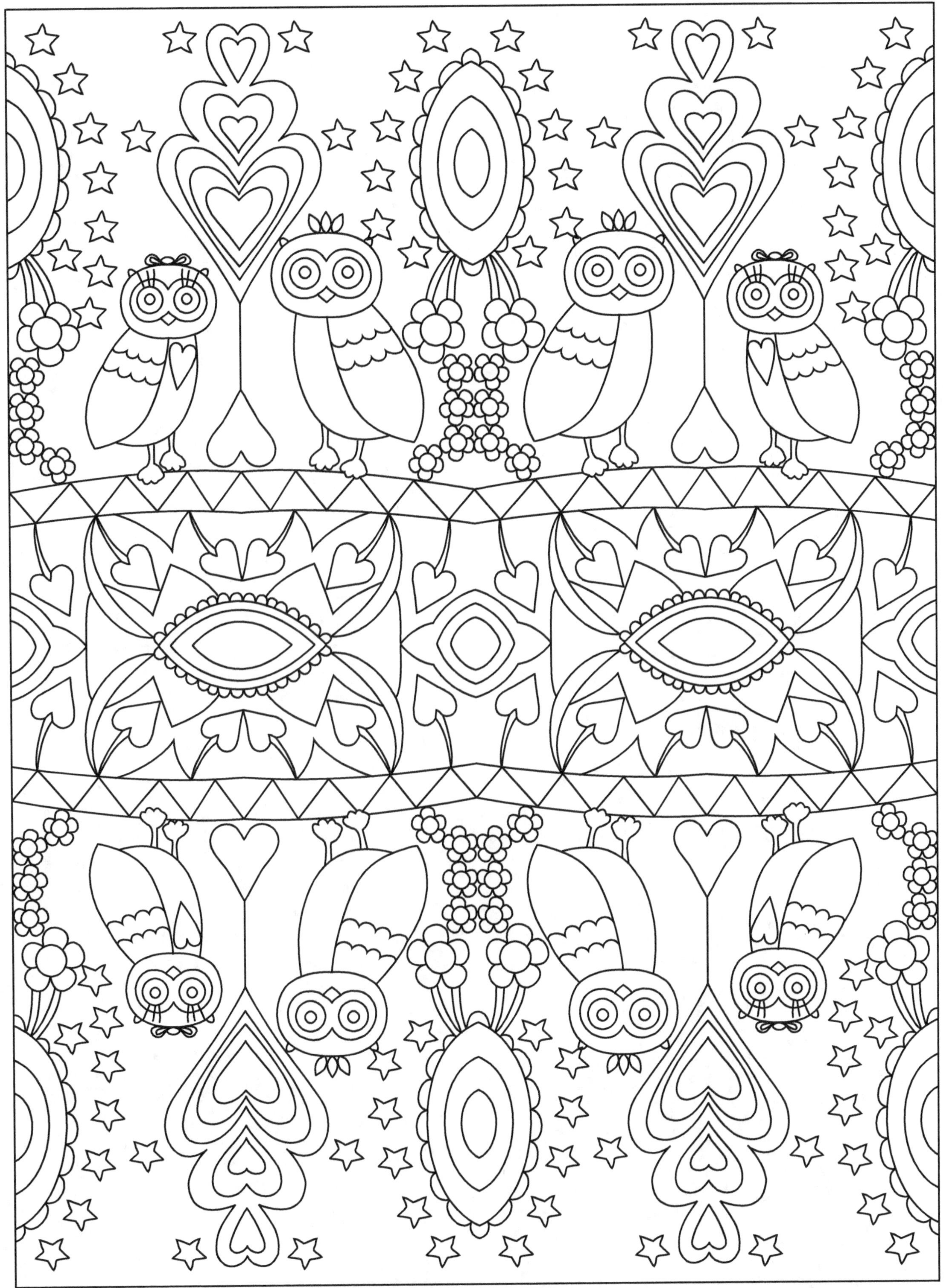

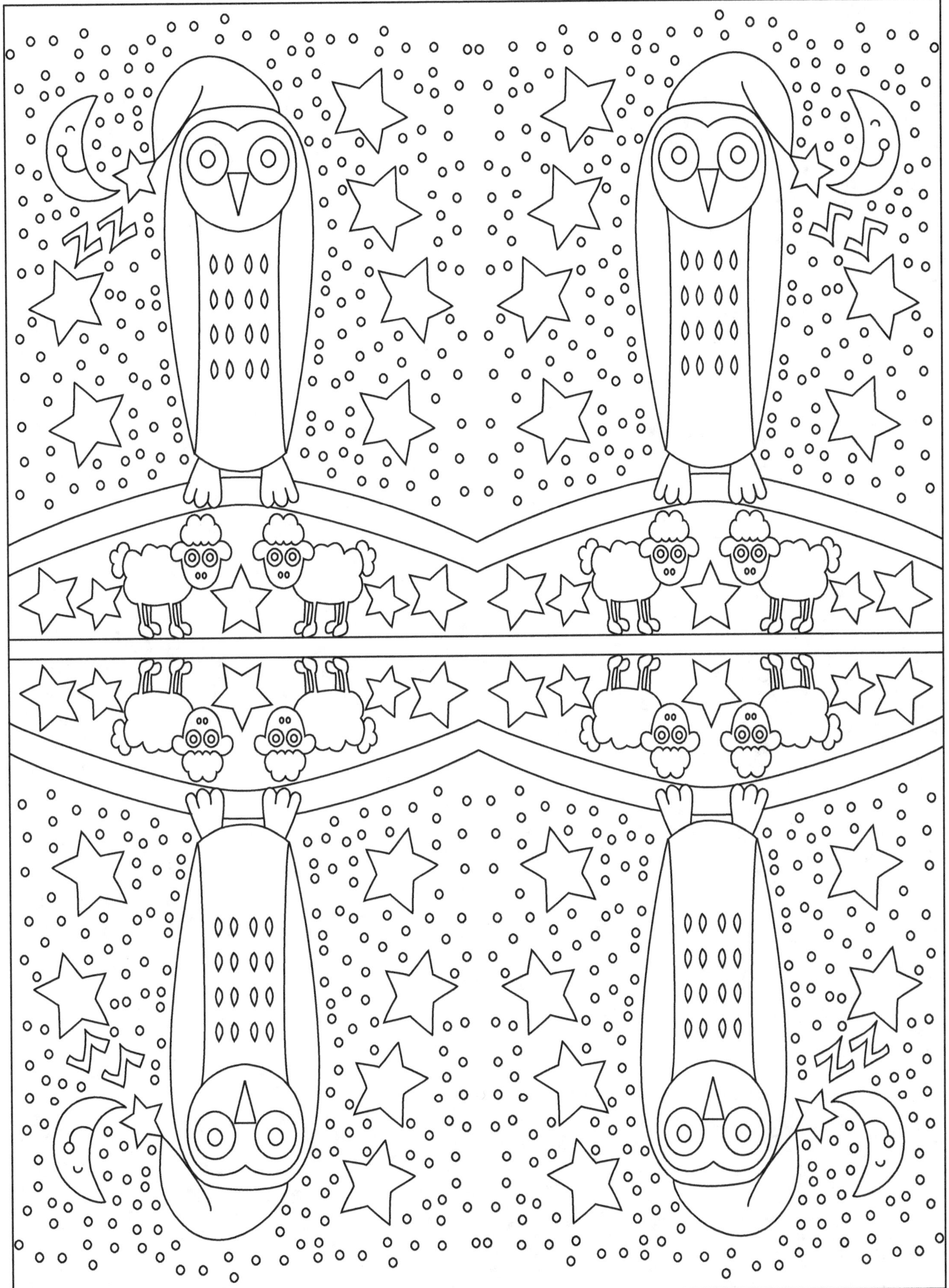

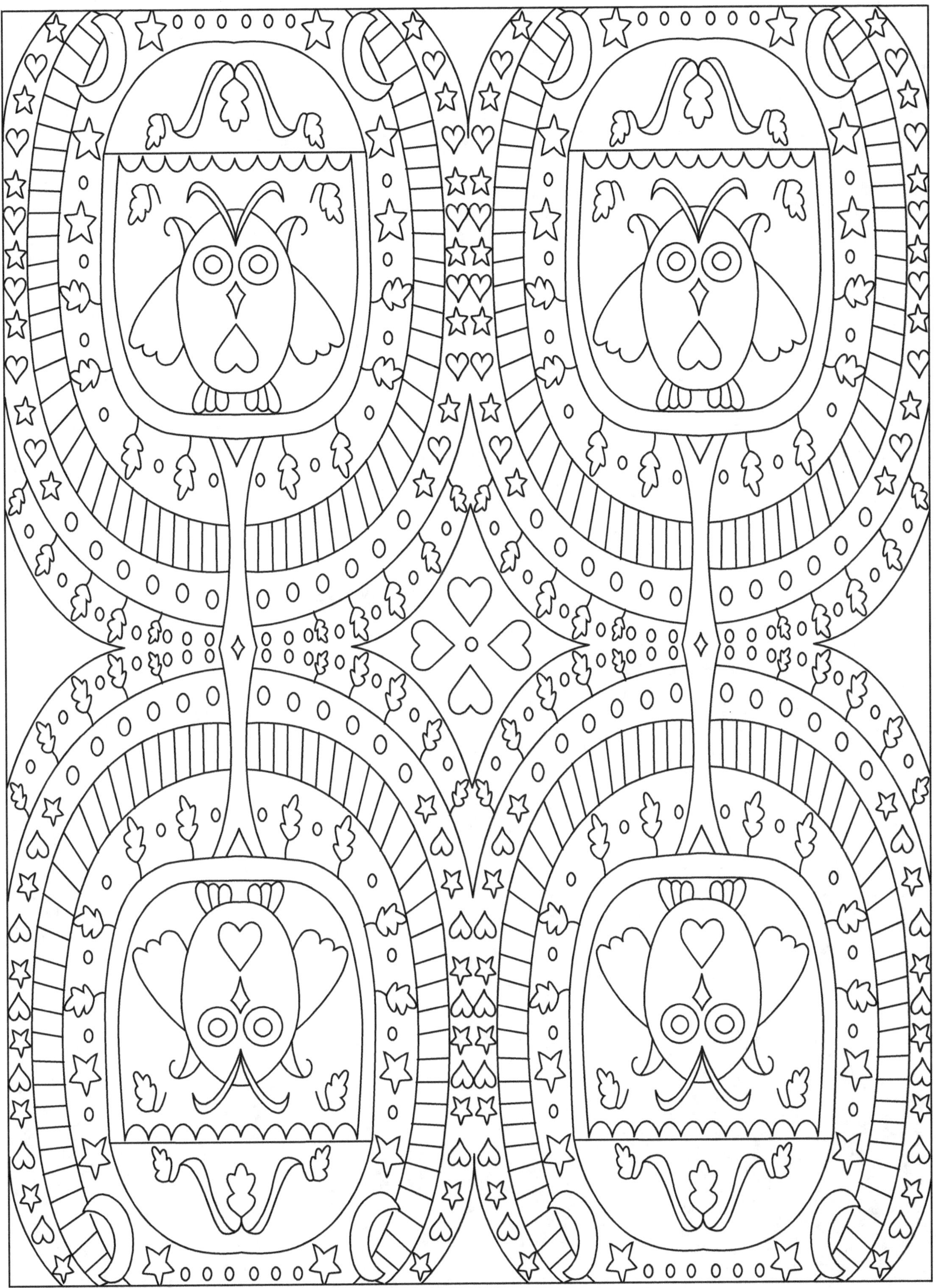

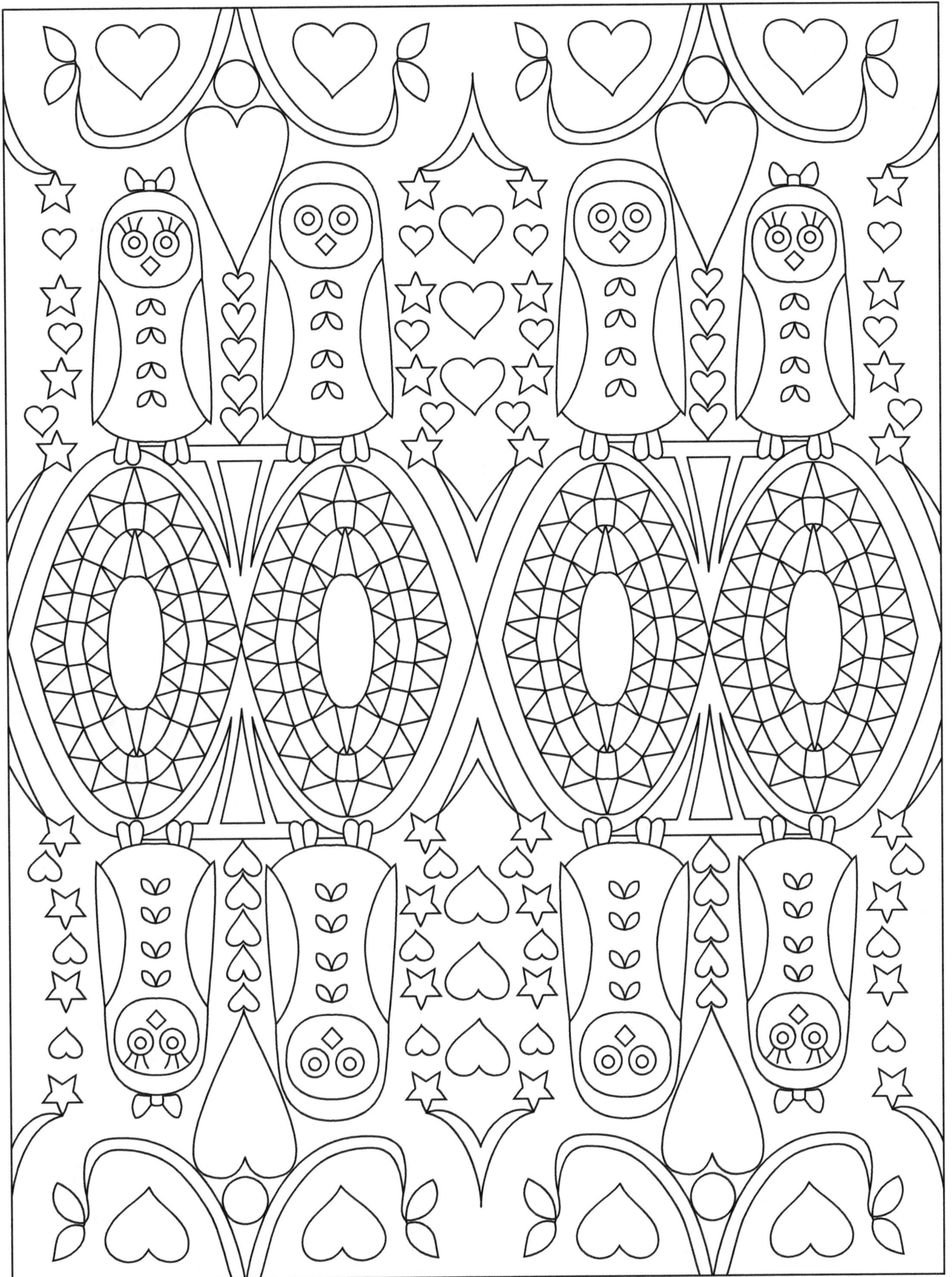

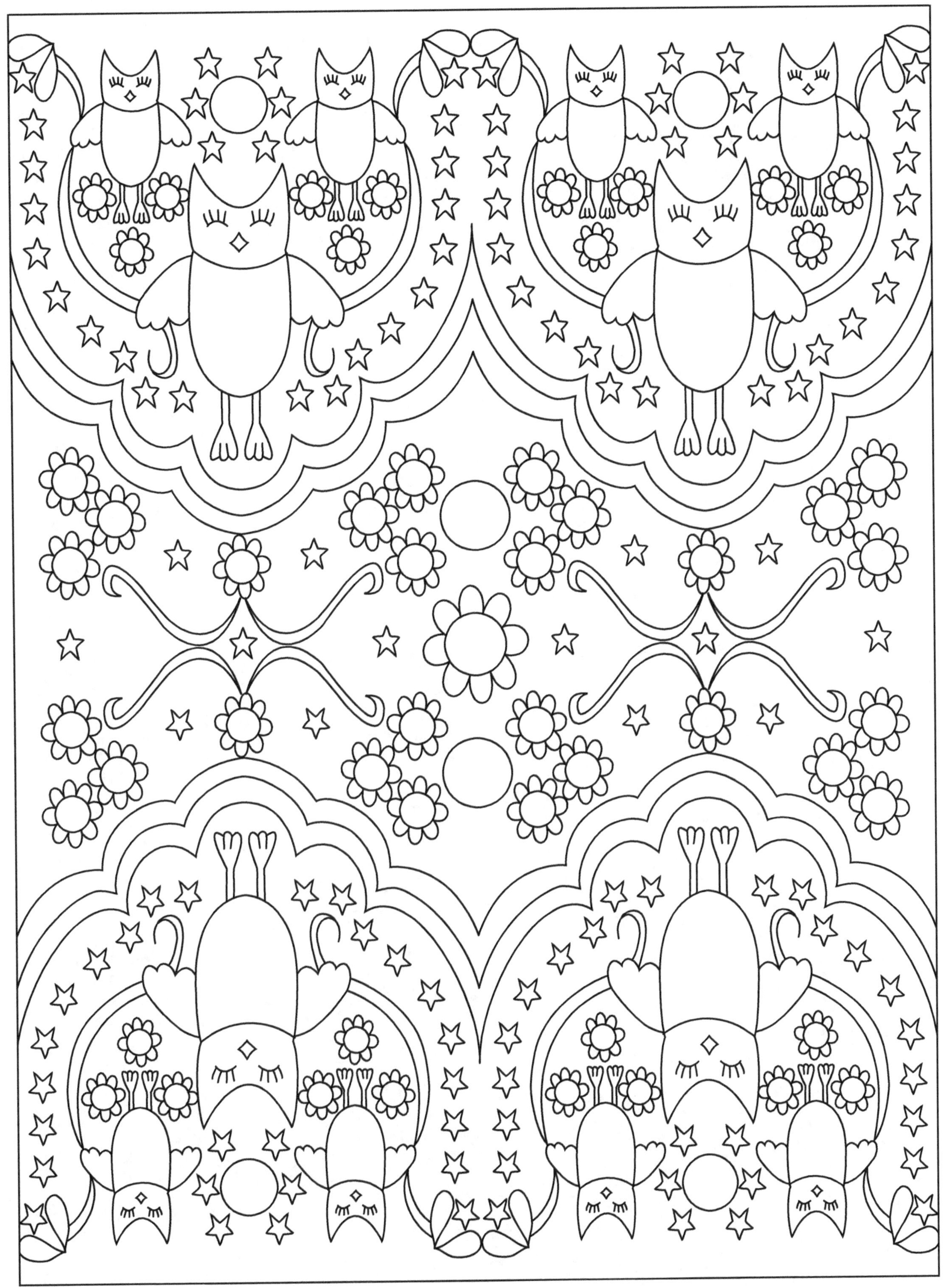

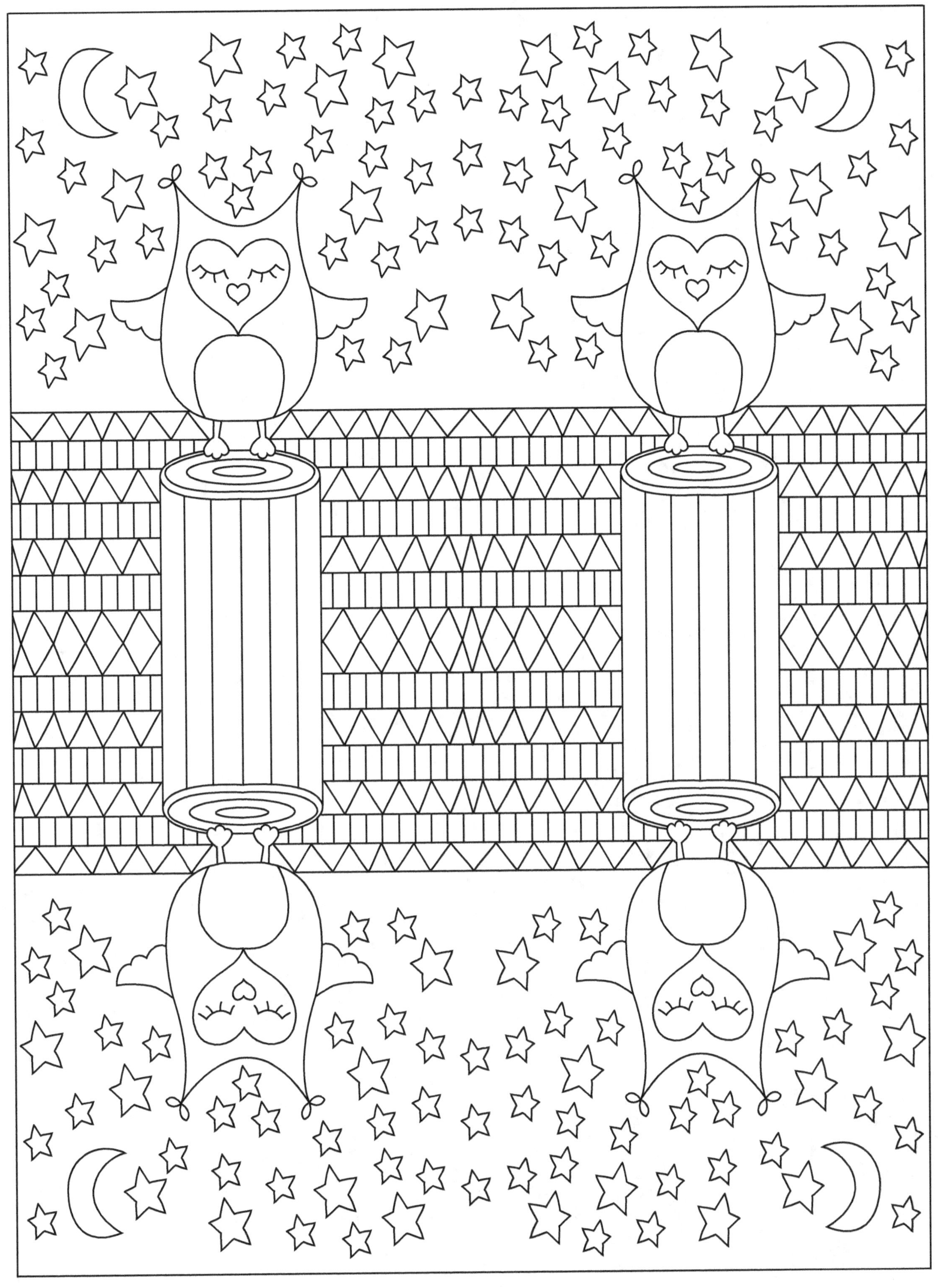

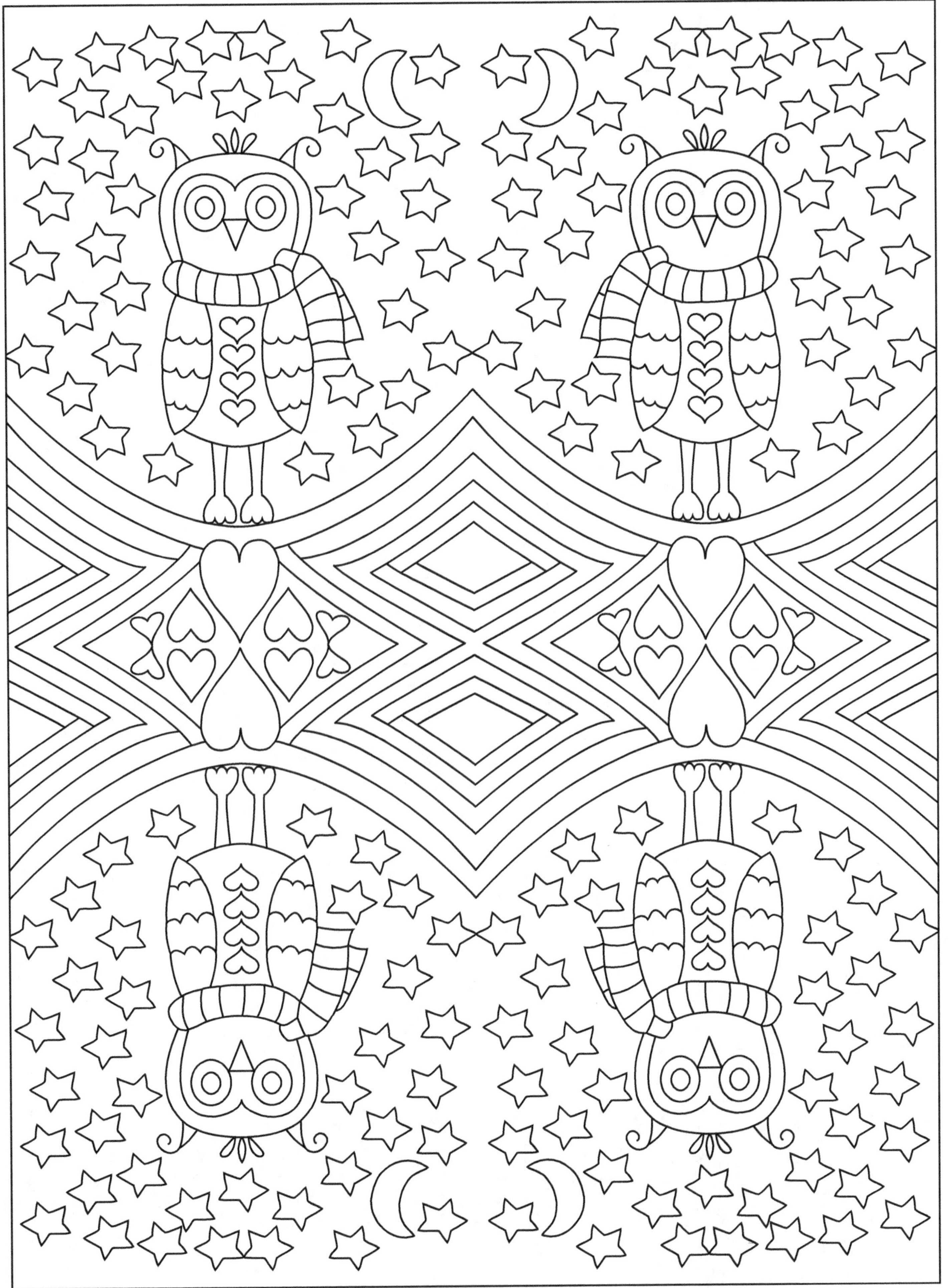

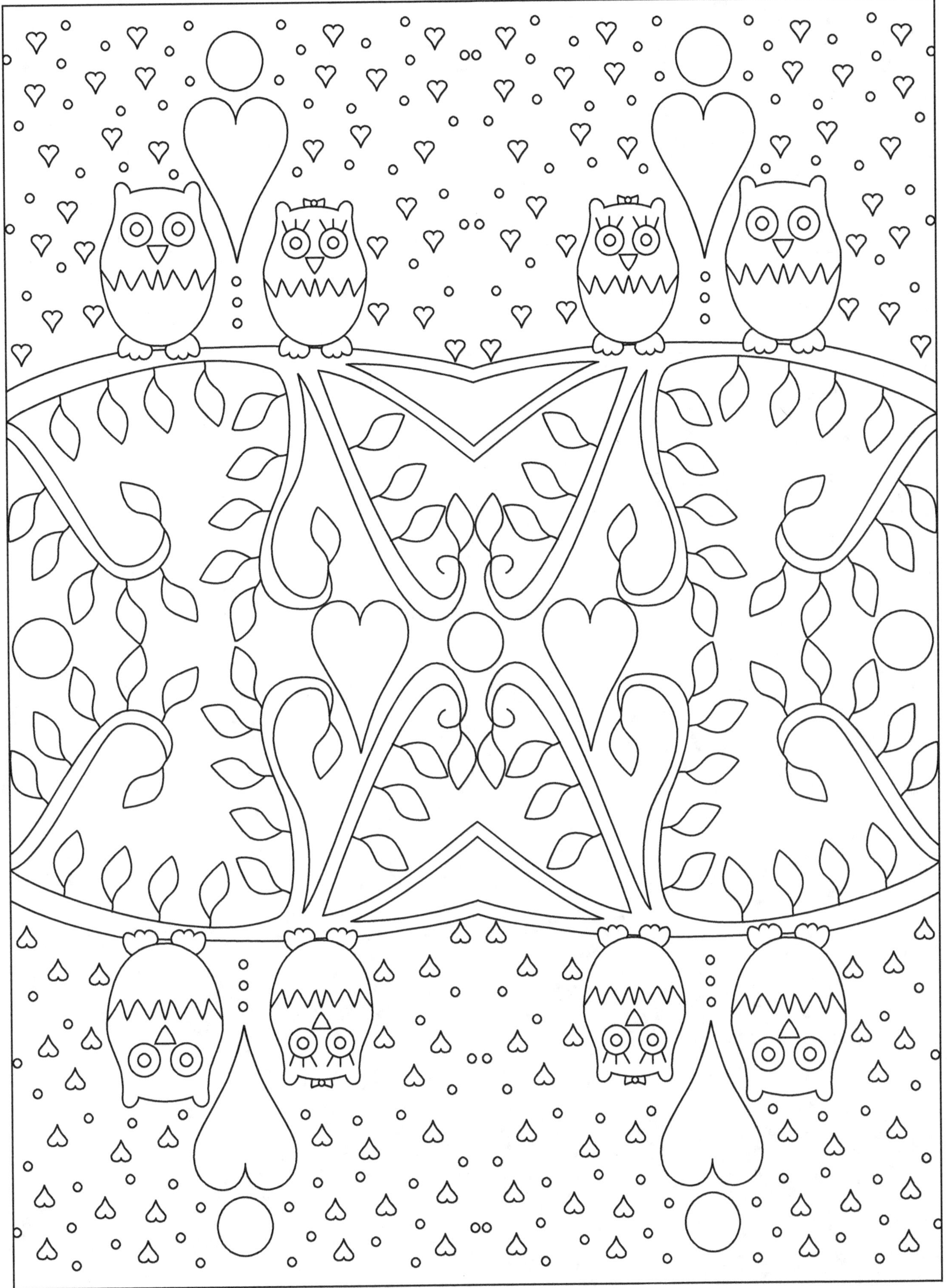

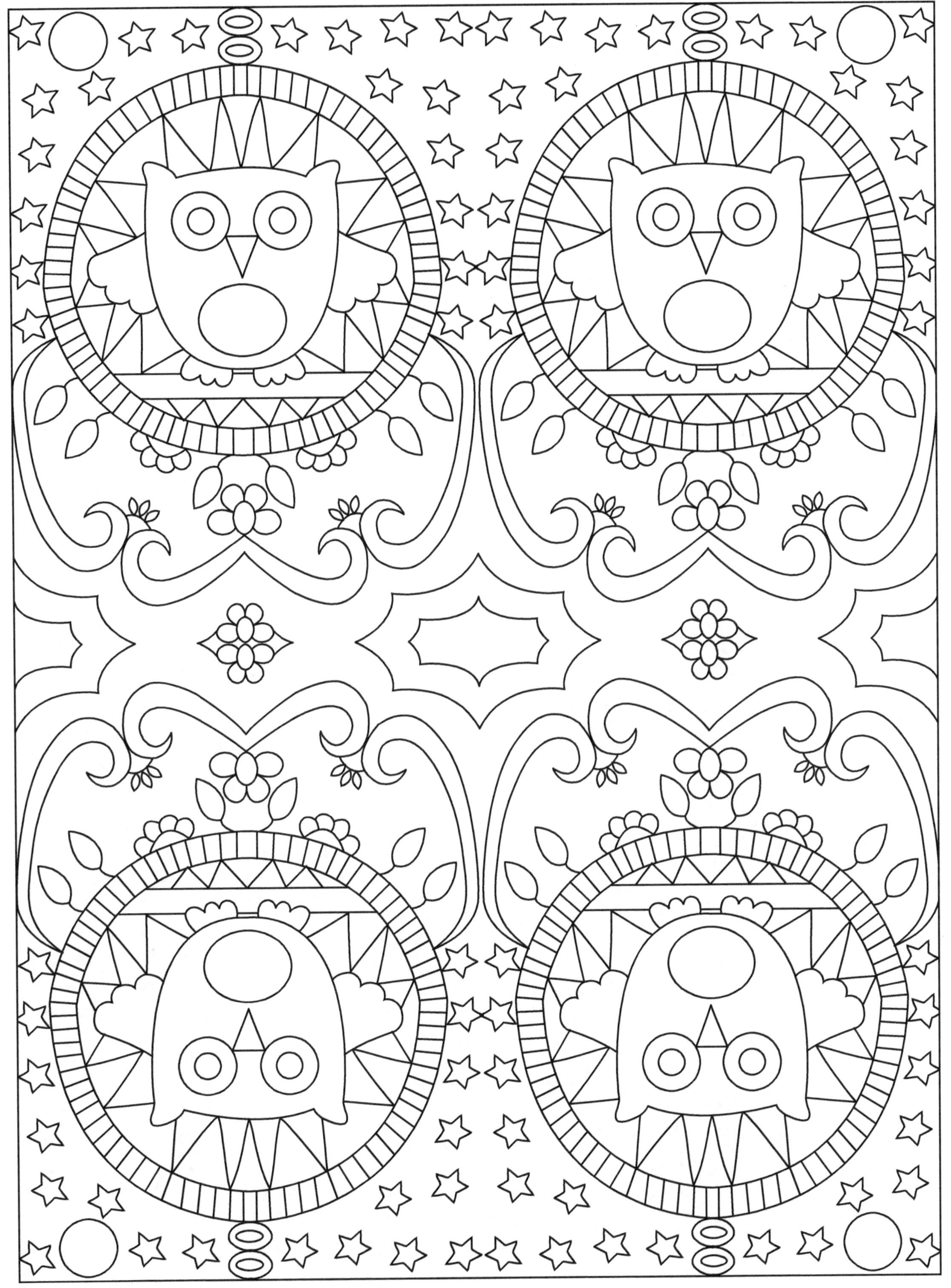

This is your test page. Use this page to test your pencils, crayons, gel pens etc. Have fun!